DISCOVERING CITY MINISTRY SECRETS
…of engaging a city and its people

By Doug Koenigsberg

D1262423

Introduction

Over thirty years ago I began my odyssey into the world of the inner city. I am still not sure I have arrived anywhere in particular, but significant mile markers have flown by. I probably know more of what NOT to do than what TO do. Perhaps I can save some time and effort for others by revealing some secrets I have discovered.

I Do Need to Set Some Boundaries

I am not trying to write crisply and LINEARLY like a good essay. What's that mean? Well, linear people tend to identify where they are and then where they want to be. If they begin at point "A" then they will look for their ultimate destination, point "Z." And just try to go straight there. Circular people look at the path and notice that it is far from straight. So they look around, smell the roses, enjoy the weather, enjoy company on the journey and are willing to simply move through 24 other points to get there. Their journeys all have stories to share and so do I.

I will be using the terms **"black" and "white"** for convenience, no pejorative intended. In my urban minority-majority world, insiders use them, and use "African American" in a formal way, nearly always around Caucasians (also their formal term). Check the context, I may also use letter abbreviations like AA for African Americans for convenience or NA for Native Americans. No abbreviations for Asian or Latino.

The street world uses the "N" word, though I rarely do so. If I say "black folk" or "black church" I am simply noting most of that group is African American of USA birth. And it is about those folks whose relatives were kidnapped and held in the USA as slaves against their will.

When I say "urban" I mean "inside the city limits, "ghetto" or where the poor, hard-living people reside; not the suburbs.

I hope to write with "some of the sand left in," that grit that gives reality to life and authenticity to this document. So don't be surprised if you are not comfortable with ALL my ideas, frankness or call-outs. I am also declining the use of footnotes, choosing to simply note the book title and author in the text. In this day of Amazon and Google, it is very easy to find a book in seconds with only that information.

I hope to use stories, narrative in the form of my story, observations and propositions to full advantage. Some stories will be embedded, but at the end of a book are my stories that don't quite fit into the body of the discussion. They are true. And they are mine. Of course, I will change names as appropriate, but the rest is what it is. Yes, my perspective is unconventional…for a simple reason. The conventional has not worked well for me!

If I am effective, this effort should find disagreement in some measure for many readers, encouragement for most and clarity for nearly all. It is primarily aimed at "white" folks, the Caucasian heritage that makes up the majority people in the USA. I think it may be useful to some minority folks, if no more than a reference in times of trouble, or even better as a "**Book to Give to Rookie White People Who are Ignorant**"

*My qualifications are a bit unorthodox. Think **journey**, **study** and **experience.***

I was a freshman at Iowa State in 1965 when I met the Navigators, fresh from an Iowa farm and a small Baptist Church. Now I am a Presbyterian Elder, though somewhat undercover at this point, in a large white suburban church. I am also ordained as an Apostolic Pentecostal Pastor in a black church, Dynamic Deliverance Cathedral, in Baltimore City -with nearly 30 years of city involvement under my belt, in my heart and in my head. It has been a long trek with a stack of failures. I have been fired, bankrupt, burned out and humiliated in more ways than I want to remember. Very high up on that stack of failure has been overall ignorance. And I really hate being stupid! As a white male from Iowa, I didn't know what I didn't know, but I was firmly convinced anyway! Much of my education, has been from trial and error. I walked the city streets mostly alone at first, or with some scruffy companions, because I could find no one who was equally ignorant but equally crazy enough to attempt the journey. For years now, my days have been infinitely flexible and subject to change. That is hard on planners. Non-cross-cultural people tend to "glaze over" quickly at the people, sights and sounds of the city, as the loud volume of a different reality quickly overcomes good intentions!!

I have done my homework; having read nearly every book I could find on cities in general and Baltimore in specific. I'm trying to be more narrative and experiential than scholarly, though I will offer references wherever it makes sense. I have tried to understand what I have seen and experienced by discussion and input from knowledgeable people.

Now About the Navigators

While this is about city ministry, at the beginning, I think it will be useful to identify my parachurch influence as well. The core comes from the Navigators, with whom I closely associate, and a couple other layers from InterVarsity Christian Fellowship. I was a full-time staffer for those organizations for nearly 20 years, working with college students in the Baltimore/D.C. area.

So what is the real-life distinctive of the Navigators? In my opinion it condenses into "**IRM**–Intentional Relational Ministry." Why the Navs in the city? Why would I care about better connections between a white group of mostly narrow-experience people (no offense intended) and all those 620,000 people in Baltimore? A distinctive has been their "Topical Memory System" in bygone years. Is there something magical about memorizing parts of the Bible? Do they do better small groups, large groups, concerts, conferences and seminars than anybody else? Do they have the best scholars and students of the Bible? The answers are generally negative to the last three questions, although it could be debated, I suppose.

What is not a debate question is the Navigators belief in the "**Worth of the Individual.**" This was captured in both the speech and writing of Dawson Trotman and any Navigator worth their salt ever since. Not only is the individual important, how they are grown, trained or "discipled" is a major pillar in the organization. At one of their conferences, the "WhingDing" in 1965, I committed myself to a pursuit of God and the engagement with people. For years now, it is about the only thing that I have been totally committed to, other than my wife and family. Even my love of flying has mostly had to take a back seat to "following God."

I have had a life-long commitment to relationships, having made relational investments in people for over 50 years. Those people were mostly on the way "**up,**" but I have also "**walked 'em down,**" that is spent time with people who were stepping or sliding slowly to personal failure. That includes friendships with people in addiction as well as professionals who were crashing. My position is that **relationships are more important than "programs."** Please note carefully that I am not excluding programming, but rather placing it in the back seat. It must be present but not in the driver seat! I think it must be evaluated for how **it promotes relationships** not the other way around. In the urban setting, we must deal with the whole person, so programs are essential, but without relationships they have a high failure rate.

I also believe the "Gospel" is **Relational** more than **Transactional**. Some have a strong narrative that highlights the cause of a separation between God and people. For them, it is all about Atonement Theory. Maybe not so much for me. The news that we can have a relationship with God easily trumps the news that we have had our spiritual legal problems resolved! Please note that I am not against programs, both programs and relationships are necessary. I am just saying that the priority should always go to "The Importance of the Individual" and the relationship to them.

My best analogy for how the Navigators work is *Flight Instruction.* Having been a pilot for more than 50 years, currently holding a Commercial license, single and multi-engine land, and an Instrument Rating. I have done some flight instruction and I am convinced it is **impossible** to teach people how to fly safely **using only** a lecture hall, classroom, video, audio or even "interactive, web-based" program . It is safest and best done one-to-one IN an airplane, with a qualified instructor. In the Air Force, when the subject of pilot training comes up, the slogan is "**There is no substitute for having air under your butt!**" or language to that effect. In my opinion, the fundamental skill of living a life in relationship to God is no different. It is best done one-to-one, in relationships with trainers, mentors and peers. First, the relationship of an instructor/mentor and then later as supportive peer relationships. While group settings may review some of the data involved, the skills needed to LIVE come from coaching and the involvement of life-on-life.

I believe that a *Flight Instruction* approach is top-of-the-line when it comes to helping people grow quickly and deeply in following Jesus. Further, strong peer relationships as co-workers are essential to the sustaining of people in ministry. As I look at the needs of the people I know in the city; *that* is the most needed input to help people change their lives. It has always baffled me a bit that some Navigator efforts seem to struggle to keep the focus on one-to-one relationships; yielding to the classroom/lecture/ seminar perhaps too often. One-to-one is clearly the main theme to their history.

I recently reread Betty Skinner's excellent efforts in her 1974 writing of the book "Daws" and noted the beginnings of the Navigators over 100 years ago with the birth of Dawson Trotman. Using my cultural eye, I note that it began as a blue collar, working class effort in the 1920's and grew upward and outward. I also note that there were no people of color in any of the pictures in the book and no thought was given to the crossing of cultures until much later, perhaps in the 1950's. This was a typical start to many of the Christian organizations at the time, so this is not meant to be criticism, just reality. However it is also a current liability.

My first contact with a memorable black person in the organization was in 1966 when I briefly met Roy Briggs. A group picture taken at the 1965 WhingDing conference shows only one black face out of the 611 men present, and if memory serves, he was an exchange student from Africa that disappeared shortly thereafter. That group was made up of college and military guys, most all of them a step or two up the cultural scale from the lumberyard of Dawson's beginnings. The understanding of the Gospel, the interpretation of the Bible and the Great Commission was mostly seen through a "rural" lens, not a "city" one, however. In my day the Navs were most effective in the "cow college," the Land Grant Universities in the Midwest. The "Farm Boys" from the 1960's and 1970's were the backbone of the Navigators rapid expansion during that time. No one made the slightest supportive reference to civil rights or Rev. Dr. Martin Luther King, or to any city political events back in the day.

In the 50 or so years since the WhingDing, there have been vast changes in the cultural Christian landscape. Today's youth are not in the same world as Dawson Trotman's day. On every front, things are different, so different that it makes no sense to even try to note all of them. There is a movement in the Nav organization to move toward the city in most parts in the world. But overcoming a rural mentality is not for the fainthearted. To do so in a legitimate way while retaining "Nav culture" has proved to be difficult.

This book is intended to be reference, a means of interaction, my contribution to people who care about the city and to those who SHOULD care. It is about my life, thoughts and interactions. But the aim is to influence the reader. I hope others can avoid common mistakes, humiliation, and sheer ignorance that I discovered along the way.

I have been given a rare treasure, but I offer an incomplete map to the reader, outlining a destination that cannot be seen from the start. For how does one see a God they do not yet know and be blessed by people they have not met?…yet.

Chapter 1

Hiding in Plain sight...
How we DON'T look at the city.

"Ah, THE CITY. It ain't no place for women, Gal, but pretty men go there."

—WC Fields, *A Fatal Glass of Beer*

Perhaps the Biggest Secret hides in plain sight. It is so common, we don't really notice**. It is the CITY itself.** We all take for granted the structure of cities, geography and the population of cities. There is the inner city, the tall buildings part of city, the sports complex, City Government, and of course the suburbs. It wasn't always this way. Jerusalem at the time of Jesus was a walled city of about 40,000. It would swell to 250,000 during festivals, but the permanent residents were estimated below 50,000. It was perhaps the largest city the New Testament Bible writers knew about. And the suburb, superhighway and speeds over 10 mph were unheard of!

In the USA, the rural (non-city) population in 1915 was about 50%. One hundred years later, In 2015, the rural population was 18%, and declining. It had been at 25% in 1990!

I think it is worth noting that in 1910, the total USA population was 92,228,496. At this writing, the USA population is 325,185,520 and climbing.

So with a bit of math, changing the percentages into numbers, the total city population in, say, 1910 was 46,114,248.

And with a bit more math, the city population now is 266,652,126… or over FIVE TIMES AS MANY PEOPLE! As I write this, I am in a city with a population of 621,849 in 2015, or roughly a 16-times-larger city than any Bible writer experienced!

Here is my assertion: if a person comes to the city with a rural, agricultural, non-city mentality, with a conservative attitude and with missiology from several decades ago, their impact may be limited! Wycliff Bible Translators and others did a great job of steering us toward a concern for "those who had not heard the Gospel in their native tongue," but somehow cities were not seen in the same way.

Now you might say, " **I live in the Suburbs**, but I am more City than Rural." Maybe, maybe not. If you only have TRANSACTIONS in the city, you may still be Rural. If your church background is Fundamentalist, Conservative, Orthodox or any other names for a similar religious views, you may be Rural in your theology. Is that wrong? Of course not. But you may have to do some detective work to understand cities and to move from "transactions" to love.

I will talk more about how to reconsider your theology a bit later, but for now, let's give some general thought to how to look at the MACRO (large) view of the city; looking to the MICRO (small) view a bit later.

MACRO CITY: *Taking the Large View*

Growing up Conservative, I was led to believe along the lines of "A Fatal Glass of Beer," that the City was an evil, Godless place, suitable only for "Evangelization." That overlooked the screamingly obvious, that people mostly CHOSE to be there. Why? Because it was a desirable place to live, work and play. Much more potential than a rural community in terms of places to live, more money to be made, and a broader selection of creature comforts. Of course, if one's desires turned to vice, that was available as well. If one aspired to be a "big frog in a big pond," the city was the place. A friend noted a few years back that it was much easier to survive as a transsexual in the city than in his rural Virginia town. So as people grouped together around their desires for living, working or playing, they developed a collective reputation. Every city has a historical trajectory which functions as a living organism. Do your know yours?

Sometimes we use an image to reframe a complex situation. I want to suggest one.

The City As Cake?

I'm a city guy. But I haven't always been, just the last 30 years or so. It may seem like a long time to you, but I live in a city that is over 350 years old, so my experience pales in comparison. For most of my 30+ years, I have struggled with ways to image what a city really is. What follows is my latest attempt.

I live in Baltimore, Maryland, so my image is the **Maryland State Dessert**, a delicacy called **"Smith Island Cake."** Normally it has multiple layers of yellow cake separated with chocolate frosting that does not spare the flavor or calories for the sake of health! We usually think of cake as a single spongy flavor covered with a single flavored frosting that may make more concessions to appearance than to taste…a la wedding cake. But not for our "City Cake." So consider the city of your reality or dream and compare it's likeness to cake! Given the diversity of the city, we must consider many layers, many shapes (not just round), multiple frostings and multiple colors.

WHAT COLOR IS YOUR CAKE?

If we are honest, the first thing that strikes us is the color. A cake may be a single or multiple colors on the outside. We all notice the melatonin present in most of the city dwellers skin. Baltimore City happens to be about 60% African American, making Baltimore a minority-majority urban center. The counties that surround it are the reverse, with the Caucasians having the majority population. The city of Baltimore hasn't always been this way. The first 300 years or so the majority was white, though there have always been minorities present somewhere even as slaves. Is this significant? Yes, because skin color is still used as a class designation in the USA society. It represents that fraction-of-a-second means of evaluation, based on learned biases.

WHAT IS THE SHAPE OF YOUR CAKE?

The shape is determined by the baker's pan, since the batter is a heavy liquid that needs guidance. Most cities have a shape that is determined by the physical features surrounding it as well as the physical features within it. Chicago, for example, came into being as a destination for floating logs. It was a lumber mill town, trees were felled in upper Wisconsin and Michigan, then floated to Chicago or rough sawn and shipped to Chicago for milling. This became attractive to the railroads and Chicago became a crossroads of rail, water and roads. To some degree it became self-generating, as it championed the "balloon construction." By changing construction engineering from "post and beam" designs to "dimensioned lumber" that was lighter and easier to build, using joists, studs, and rafters, with hollow walls; that style of construction is in vogue today. More housing at lower prices lead to the expansion of industrial refining and manufacturing so lumber took a back seat in Chicago. Later, changes in demand and shifts in transportation diminished manufacturing, and led to the closing of the Stockyards with their accompanying slaughterhouses and the demise of the steel mills. Now Chicago is more of a financial and commerce center, small manufacturing accompanied with the consequences of sub-urbanization.

Shape has great influence of the layers of our cake since it has history and trajectory behind it. Looking again at the shape can be very important because we tend to be given a piece of cake without necessarily being aware of the whole it came from. Baltimore is an old city with a lot of history. We recently celebrated the role of the efforts of Francis Scott Key in writing what is now our National Anthem. The State of Iowa, where I grew up, was not even in existence at that time and would not be for another 50 years or so. Baltimore was over 150 years old when Iowa became a state, but still more of a small town than a city.

Draw the outline of your favorite city on a piece of paper and note how the outline and surrounding geography has effected what happens INSIDE those lines. I note that Washington, D.C. is only 30 miles away and the gravity field from it influences Baltimore. But a bit like a step-sister. Baltimore has always been a working town, blue collar and rough. Washington, D.C. …not so much. Washington D.C. builds word pictures, Baltimore builds everything from horseshoes to automobiles to airplanes.

What about the Flavor of your city/cake? What about the Style? What about the Layers?

The National Museum of African American History and Culture, next to the Washington Monument in Washington, D.C. has a great quote by George C. Wolfe, "God Created Black People and Black People Created STYLE!" Baltimore has a lot of black flavor and lots of style. But that has been repressed.

Baltimore, my city, has always been shaped by white people despite other layers of cake and frosting. It was heavily influenced by slavery, surrounded by plantations and having "slave houses" built near larger upper class houses. It has always been segregated to some degree.

So, who is in control?

Looking at the base layer of the Baltimore cake, we see that whatever the color of the mixture, the bottom layer is controlled both in shape and substance by white people. In fact, I don't know of a United States city *that isn't "owned"* at least in terms of real estate, by white-skinned people. It may be held by corporate entities, but most of those stockholders are white. No indictment intended at this point, just suggesting that property ownership as well as many other factors that shape and form the foundation of a city are significant to our understanding of the cake. Which starts us off with a base layer…

Real Estate as the Foundation Layer

As Europe emptied its streets, byways and prisons of undesirable people by shipping them to America, they encountered Native Americans who seemed to have little desire to lay claims to real property, in stark contrast to Europe. They had some sensitivity to how it was used and protested their subsequent exclusion from it, but the white folks (with firepower) could bring their notions of possession which overcame the protest at the price of Native American lives if they resisted. Indeed, the land was in many cases "claimed" for some member of royalty or privilege through the actions of sponsored invaders. Where I grew up, Iowa, was first claimed by France, then Spain, then claimed again by Napoleon of France and then "purchased" by the

United States Government and resold or given to white people. Recently I examined the Abstract of Title for our farm there. It came into being in 1856 as a grant to a person and everyone following can "sell" it to others. Indeed, Dad acquired that farm from an estate in 1943 and retained his claim until his passing. It is the use of a piece of real estate that determines the rest of the cake. Though somewhat rare, sometimes structures erected on a real property have to be torn down because the ownership and usage is not proper. But in any case, land claims of the European "squatters" have been upheld…by people with a vested interest in the ownership! Baltimore is home to a Federal Court!

Indeed, the rights to own land, particularly one's home, has been fundamental to the mindset of Americans. Watching "cowboy movies" from almost the inception of "moving pictures," it was nearly always about land and protecting the rights of a "rightful owner" even though such owners were never completely right… according to the people who were already here.

The Next Layer of the Cake Is About Land Use.

The people in the city need jobs. That is why most of their ancestors moved or stayed here. The rural minded folks moved West, some to escape other people and some for the way of life. But most of the people just wanted to work, raise a family, care for them and enjoy time away from work. Over the years the land use may change, as it did in Chicago. But it is the employment that dictates the rest of the city functions.

Here is a list of many of the functions that characterize a city. Notice how many of the are about human relationships… concerning the success, failure or continuance of them.

LEGAL—*Courts, Laws, Police, Injustice or Justice*

HOUSING—*Public or Private, Owned or Rental, Rich or Poor*

MEDICAL—*Doctors, Hospitals, Nursing Homes, Rehab, Insurance, Institutions*

EDUCATION—*Elementary, Middle, High, Colleges, Universities, Institutes, Seminaries, Nursing, Technical Schools*

NON-PROFITS—*Churches, Schools, Seminaries, Community Orgs, NGO's (non-governmental organizations)*

ENTERTAINMENT—*Theaters, Stadiums, Field Houses, Shows, Sports Venues, Race Tracks*

GOVERNMENT—*Utilities, Oversight, Laws, Licensing, Infrastructure, Prominent Features*

FOODS—*Cafes, Groceries, Restaurants, Food Trucks, Corner Markets, Wholesale, Retail, Raw Or Cooked*

EVENTS—*Meetings, Tragedy, Celebrations, Traditions, Historical Commemorations*

FINANCIALS—*Insurance, Banking, Financing, Money Flow*

MANUFACTURING—*From Printing to Processing to Packaging to Paperwork to the Conversion of Raw Materials into Goods.*

Commerce at the Core

All these have one thing in common. They **represent jobs**. So the people in a city need income to enjoy the functions of a city. All along the way, people get paid or receive income in some manner that allows them to live, sleep, eat and enjoy life to some degree. Rich or poor, white collar or blue,

So what is the next layer on your cities cake? Look over the above list and pick several of the functions to stack on YOUR cake.

THE CITY IS ALL ABOUT HUMAN RELATIONSHIPS.
That binds all the layers together People live in cities because of the proximity of what they desire. In the case of Baltimore, several of the layers have white frosting between. The white folks control the real estate, much of the manufacturing, most of the financial, oh well, most everything, although there has been some delegation in education, non-profits, and city government. But those folks live in the surrounding county, not the city. Baltimore is 60% black. So as you move around in the cake, there are large areas that are flavored by black people, surrounding or on top of the white layers.

White people own the baseball and football franchises in Baltimore, but many the players (workers) are black. So the student of the city has to move about INSIDE the cake to understand it. Understanding is required. Where there is not a good understanding of the cake, there are problems, not unlike the Baltimore Uprising in 2015 which was about the people of Baltimore deciding they had had enough of the Police misconduct. To be heard or understood, they had to raise a fuss.

As you think about your city, see if you can make use of the City as Cake. What are the layers? Look at the inter-relationships. What are those characteristics? What about Style, Flavor and land use?

Before we get too far along in looking at the possible structure and secrets of a city, I think we should identify our own secrets.

CHAPTER 2

WHAT IS YOUR SECRET...?

What Draws You To A City?
Where Are You In Your Understanding?
Why Would You Read a Book Like This?

Having been around city ministry for over 30 years, I have had the opportunity to hear from others as well as consider my own motivations. For most people, myself included, the story begins with noticing the NEEDS of the city. Almost without exception, black, white, Asian or Latino, people begin with the negatives:

- CRIME STATISTICS
- RACISM
- EDUCATION
- BEGGING
- MEDICAL NEEDS
- POLITICS
- CHILDREN AT-RISK

- POVERTY
- ALIENATION
- HOMELESSNESS
- HUNGER
- DRUGS *(non-prescription, non-pharmaceutical)*
- ABANDONED HOUSES
- INCARCERATION

What Are Your Needs...
That Make You Want To Engage A City?

"Great Commission Obedience"... The desire to straighten out someone else's life

To make money .... The desire to straighten out broken systems

A heart for people............ The desire to make a difference with your life

A new idea .... To be with friends

Curiosity.................... Finding the good in people

Here is my key secret: The lasting motivation, which may take years to appreciate, is **to find God in His people there**. They live and experience a part of God that you simply cannot know from the outset. If you only look at the needs, you will miss it. You must learn **the assets of God's church in the city and let those people care for you**! In the end it is your need to know God and walk in Fellowship this side of death that can sustain you.

It is not necessary to completely understand this at the outset. Indeed, time and maturity is the prerequisite. But a desire to deal with racism is required.

If you were born after 1990 or so, your experience with racism is likely to be very different from mine. You may be familiar with the words:

- SOCIAL CAPITAL
- BIAS
- DISCRIMINATION
- WHITE PRIVILEGE
- PATERNALISM
- INSTITUTIONAL RACISM
- CULTURAL BLINDNESS
- RACISM IN GENERAL

But do you understand the impact that is behind them? As you look around and try to place yourself on some continuum that recognizes both issues of class and race, where might you be? Perhaps it will be useful to look at my journey.

Because crossing into an urban sub-culture is a stretch for upper and middle class people, perhaps it is reasonable to ask where I am now and how I got here. As I look over my shoulder, I see that there were STAGES that I seem to have gone though. Those stages are not unlike stages of grief/healing. I see seven of them to this point. While your stages might vary and you might not start in the same place, nevertheless, here is my perspective and experience simplified:

My Seven Stages (so far!)

1. **Seeing People As Objects.**
   I began by describing people of color as *"Them* and *Those"* and with a single descriptor. *"Those people are (fill in your worst descriptive term)."* Most white folks have a single word or two to describe all people of darker color. In fact, my grandparents called them "darkies." I also heard the term 'colored'! I remember as a Sophomore in college, hearing of the death of Rev. Dr. Martin Luther King, Jr., and saying out loud to myself, "Maybe those (colored)people will calm down now" On more than three occasions, I have visited his grave in Atlanta and each time, through some bitter tears, have said, "I'm sorry, I didn't know…I didn't know…" He was not my "people" in those days. I didn't even know how foolish that sounded!

2. **Feeling Sorry For Certain People.**
   Then I read John Howard Griffin's "Black Like Me." That one got my attention. A few years later, I listened to a young black college student describe how, when he was young, he would practice in front of a mirror for hours on end, hoping he could learn to hold

his lips so they wouldn't look so big. He wanted to look more "white." I was stunned. I could not believe that our US culture would do that to one of its own, letting him know that he was not good enough just as he was, but, clearly, it did. I felt guilty about and sorry for African-Americans, in how our culture has wounded them. Grippingly sorry. It was OK to feel sorry for the "Heathen in Africa" and to pray for missionaries "laboring in the foreign fields" when I was growing up, but it was a puzzle to consider people of color within the USA.

3. **Getting a Desire to Actually Know Certain Groups of People.**
I realized my near-total ignorance of black folk in the USA. That was unacceptable to me, so I worked hard at building relationships. I am sorry to my core, now, that I put my black friends through the torture of my questions, but I knew no other way. I have a great many people to thank for that, hopefully I can mention at least a few at the end of this writing effort. My revelation was that in the same way I could recognize the class and role of certain white folks, with study and effort I could do the same for people of color. It became worth doing as I moved toward the city.

4. **Having a Desire to *BE LIKE* Them, but *NOT BE* them.**
The move from seeing a **people group** as a mere object worthy of study to being **people** to emulate is a major one. In his book, *The Tanning of America* subtitled *How Hip-Hop created a culture that rewrote the rules of the new economy,* Steve Stoute comments on the fact that hip-hop music was purchased in greater amounts by white folks than black. He attributes some of this to "Polyculturalism," that development on the part of white youth to learn about and appreciate the highlights of another culture. Even in my own kids like a variety of cultural foods, can converse with a variety of ethnic people, and have nothing bad to say about others. That doesn't automatically make them non-racist, just easier to get along with!! Perhaps the enjoyment of a culture's benefits is not acceptance, just toleration. I know of no white person who would like to BE black in the USA! If a drug or surgical procedure could make white people a dark black person, I don't think it would be in demand! That should say something right there.

5. **Having the Desire to *BE WITH* Them.**
In church, work, play, just hanging out, most anyplace. I remember watching the movie, "Glory" and identifying with the character Col. Robert Gould Shaw, played by Matthew Broderick, a white Lieutenant. He is killed in a Civil War battle along with the all-black regiment he commanded during a suicide mission. At the end of the movie, the burial detail picks him up and rolls him

into a mass grave with the rest of his men. By now I had strongly identified with this character, with a great passion that surprised me, I said to myself, in not quite in these words, "Bury me with the (black people)." It was something of a surprise to me, for I had not known how deep my identification was at that point. But 30+ years in a middle-class black neighborhood has had an effect. I still claim it is the best kept secret in the world, the benefits of being white in a black neighborhood.

6. Hanging My Heart There.

Every chance I get, I tell the folks at Dynamic Deliverance Cathedral, "My body may need to go elsewhere, but my heart stays here" I miss the world of black folk greatly when I am away from them. Being around all white people for more than a few days wears on me. I don't feel at home surrounded by all whites. I really feel like I am a city insider looking out rather than a white man looking in. That is true in a general statement with exceptions; obviously I love my wife, children, family and all my white friends! But I cannot live where there are no black people. I want to live under the "Cover" of a black Bishop, black immediate supervisor, and black senior leadership in the Navigators. Nothing against white folks, I just have my preferences.

7. Never Wanting to Leave.

I cannot imagine what it is like to hang your heart in a place and then be forced to leave. At this point, I am old and have means; I'm not moving!

Somewhere in the middle of my stages, I realized the biggest secret of all. I was receiving much more than I was giving out. That God himself was rewarding me by showing the parts of Him that were present in city people. It is no sacrifice when you get more than you give! In every area of my life as I tried to give out, I eventually got back many times more than I put in. God began to bless my family, finances and most of all, our relationship to Himself.

So, I never felt a call, even as I moved from stage to the next. Possibly I wouldn't have known what that meant even if I got one. Perhaps the real core of the "call" to something is preceded by a lack of faith. Since I didn't know the sheer magnitude of what I didn't know, I simply kept moving in the direction that seemed open to me. I gave up the need to foretell the future and concentrated on being a servant. No great virtue here, just pragmatics. What was the alternative to serving God? That had no appeal. I just followed my heart and served wherever that led.

I think there is a point of no return to crossing cultures. At some point, you can get to where you can never go back to a position of ignorant bliss... because you simply don't want to. If you are one of the fortunate, you may never have to. If my "heart" battery needs recharging, I can get it quicker from the city and its people than the county these days. Please note that I am not excluding white folk here. I still love the country and all the white friends across the years. But I see things from a bigger picture and it is BOTH black and white, along with some other tones! But my beloved Baltimore City, my instructor and teacher for the past 32 years, is majority non-white.

However, YOU might also be at a secret fork in the road of engaging a city. I hope this book will help you to recognize that. As well as some pitfalls, like:

Setting People on Fire

I tried to establish a rapport with people in the inner-city neighborhood by being helpful, back in my landlord days. I tried to connect with the teens I knew from the street who were facing a challenging future. So when I saw the kids across the street from one of my apartment buildings having a problem trying to start a small dirt bike, it caught my attention.

I was done for the day, in fact it was almost dark. I knew some of the pre-teens by face, one of two by name, so I grabbed my tools and I pitched in. Without saying much.

I could smell gas, in fact it was dripping out of the carburetor. I removed the spark plug, so I could check the spark. I stood up, turned on the switch and kicked the kick starter.

A blast of gasoline shot out the spark plug hole, more than I expected, and the spark plug suddenly decided to cooperate by......sparking. This sent a stream of flaming gasoline directly......onto the kid holding the handlebars for me. He quickly decided to focus his attention on putting out his flaming leg and danced away, vocalizing his discomfort. Meantime, the burning fuel expanded to other places and increased in intensity. This caused the other participants to back some distance away, leaving me with the fire.

I grabbed a can of "Fix a Flat" out of my van nearby, which I believed had a watery substance that would help put out the fire. Which it might have contained, except the propellant in the can turned out to be propane! So the more of it I sprayed, the greater the flames! With that sudden realization, I followed the lead of everyone else, I backed away also!

Now all of this happened in a residential area with Baltimore rowhouses on either side of the street. That meant my audience, both on the steps outside and in the second-floor windows might well have exceeded 100 people. The screams of the burning kid had no doubt recruited additional observers.

Not far away, the sounds of the Baltimore City Fire Department had begun. Someone had the good sense to call in the burning dirt bike. Unsure of what my best options were, I stayed put, but made no moves that would attract attention to myself. I sat on some vacant steps nearby. The fire truck came blasting up, parking in the street next to the burning motorbike. Slowly, one or two firemen got out of the truck, got a small hose and put out the fire. A man got out of the truck with a clipboard and asked loudly, "Does anyone know who owns this?"

I certainly did not know the owner and no one else came forward with the requested information, so I maintained my silence ... along with a studied look of disinterest. After a few minutes, the firemen drove off, leaving a wet, smoking hulk of a dirt bike for someone. I could see little point of my presence, so I soon followed the example of the firemen. The next day, when I returned, the bike was gone. Even tho people knew who I was, no one said anything about the kid I set on fire. Sometime later, we all laughed about it, but I thought about it from time to time.

I think the lesson, which I still struggle to learn, is about involvement. As the WMOTS, (White Man On The Scene) I assumed the situation requested my assistance. I had the knowledge, or at least I thought I did, to assist someone I wanted to impress. But perhaps the community would have been better served if I had NOT nominated myself to be a motorcycle mechanic. Perhaps the kids would have learned more if they had continued to work on the bike themselves. Had I been successful, they would simply have ridden the dirt bike illegally up and down the street until they crashed, or were caught by the Police or it failed. That would not have improved the neighborhood. So at this point in time, I don't do that kind of thing anymore.

I wait to be invited. If I act as a WMOTS, I assume a role that separates me from the neighbors. I don't want to do that. In fact, that is a lesson ALL white folks should learn. It is mannerly to be asked for assistance, not to assume your assistance is required. It is not really "serving" when you don't seek permission. It is just rude. Dare I say it? Even racist.

I know this might seem like a hard thing to hear. But it might prevent flaming kids in the future!

Do You Have a Secret Desire to Fix Things?

I went to a small group meeting one night which was about city ministry. The presenter outlined all the groups which the church supported who had a "mission" in Baltimore. There was some pride in noting the 10 to 13 groups who benefited from the largess of the congregation. Those groups were reaching out to meet certain perceived needs in the largely minority black city, not too far from the church. I should have kept my mouth shut, I suppose. Instead I said, "I notice that ALL the groups we support were started by white people. **What do we support that was initiated by black people?**" The answer, of course, was none.

Since then, that church has made some slow but significant changes; moving to back the initiative of a couple young city churches.

The fork in the road is, **Who initiates, controls, staffs and manages city outreach? Is it to be invented IN THE CITY or is it invented IN THE SUBURBS?** That has a major effect on the first myth.

It seems to me that the white Christian world still struggles to accept, credit and serve under black leadership. How do you give authority to someone you think is needy? **Welcome to paternalism!**

In contrast, think of how quick you give authority to someone *Who Has What You Want!* What if something you greatly desire is possessed by a person of color? Will you submit to them…to get what they have?

Scary thoughts? I hope so.

But the secret, that only you know, is your answer to the question, *Where Are You Now?* If you can answer that, you are off to a good start.

Door Bump

It started in the parking lot at Sam's Club. I drove in, somewhat absent-mindedly, opened my door and let it swing. It made a thump when it hit the mirror of the car beside me.

"Hey, what is with you?" an angry voice said from 20 feet away. The voice belonged to a young African-American man who was standing with his mother. "That is a new car!"

I noticed the temporary license plate and realized it was a very new car. Caught off guard, I said, "it didn't hurt anything, it just hit the side mirror!"… as tho it made a difference WHERE one's car was struck.

"Can't you even say you're sorry?' came the reply.

My mumbled, "sorry," didn't really impress him, and I was walking away anyway. So much for racial reconciliation…

So why was I so unprepared to respond correctly?

My instant response was driven by values. I have always considered a car to be transportation, amusement or entertainment. I have bought and sold over 50 of them in my time, including the purchase of several new ones … and lots of junkers. Dents, scratches, bangs, bumps and small impacts don't trigger much of a reaction in me. In fact, once I had two car accidents in one day! Recently I drove a co-owned 2006 Corvette Convertible for 18 months… mostly because it cost me so little, yet seems to impress people so much. To me it is just a 10-year-old Chevy. After all, it is just a car, a money pit, one of the greatest drains of personal net worth ever invented.

What was HIS value? What did a car mean to him? Large segments of our society have a love affair with cars and they are symbols of a variety of things. For many people, their best or worst memories have something to do with cars. For others, a car symbolizes economic attainment. Some suggest that the most major evidence of a move OUT of poverty is a car. For some, the car is their major possession. They are more likely to act out in road rage, to defend their car with their life or to seek vengeance on people who disparage their car.

Of course, I had my own justification of why my banging his mirror was no big deal. As a white male, large and in-charge, I was not empathetic or even cognizant. I was lost in the fog of my own mind and white privilege gave me an excuse. You see, I really don't have to be bothered much with the feelings of minorities. Oh, I can say the words of empathy or apology, but I don't have to mean them. I just don't have to care.

My mischievous wife made a crude sign that sits on the window over my desk as I write this. It reads. **"I understand……I don't care!"** She is trying to highlight my understanding, but also my lack of compassion. As a white man, I don't need compassion, I have privilege.

I have insurance on my car with a very minimal deductible. I have access to either credit or money that will allow me to buy any car I want, most any time I want. But I like the idea of investing capital, so both my main cars (at the time) have over 130,000 miles and are unremarkable. I don't have to love a car. Or even care.

So who wins the door bump battle? I do. At least on a pragmatic level. On a spiritual or racial level, I clearly don't. "Each of you should look not only on your own interests but also on the interests of others" Phil 2:4 To be honest, I assumed he was NOT my brother in Christ. He was, after all, a young black man, probably in between confrontations with Police. Right? No, that instinct is wrong.

Thankfully, the car bump occurred some years ago. **These days I am more likely to assume he is a brother in Christ than not.** I discovered that if I assume black people are followers of Jesus, I am much more likely to be correct than to assume otherwise. Still, I am a recovering racist, not a cured one. I have the option to care. And I do. I chose to understand the other person's values and appreciate them. And next time be more careful.

Chapter 3

6 MYTHS ABOUT *NEED*

The concept of NEED, that deficiency we detect in other people or situations, deserves a closer look. Perhaps the perception of need in others allows us to mask the needs we have deep in our soul?

MYTH 1: You Need a Special Call to *Minister In The City*

Really? Does that make sense? It is a little like saying **you need to have a "call" to be a sports fan**! If you care about baseball, for example, you are free to pick any team you like and be their "fan." That entitles you buy tickets to the game, scream in the stands while wearing a team jersey, slap goofy stickers on your car and watch your team on TV for hours on end. What was the reason? Because you cared about baseball.

Now if you *say* you care about baseball, but have no team that you support, what would that mean? "Oh, I just like baseball in general, even tho I never go to a game, don't buy memorabilia, never watch it on TV or have favorite players." Would you be believable?

So Why Do You Need a "Call"?

I run into people who have some elaborate story about how "God told them" to start a church, "Minister to the homeless," feed the starving, etc. I notice that many of them quietly fade away over the years. Somehow, having a "call," while irrefutable by me, is not particularly permanent, I guess.

In fact, the notion of a "call" is not universal; many people performed certain functions in the Bible with no reference to a "call." Yes, Jesus called the 12 to be his "Disciples." Paul was zapped by the light while on a road trip and responded to further "calls" later. But most people, particularly the ones who never made it into the Bible record, simply responded to their heart as it was prompted by the Spirit. We know little of the "70" that were the next group in addition to the 12 disciples. Or the heroes of Hebrews 11, later in the chapter. They were just being obedient.

Perhaps you do need **a *Major*, a *Major* call to initiate a group outside the city, parachute in some pioneers, buy a nice church building, organize**

a youth program and set up shop. But those calls have not proven out as well as their press releases would suggest.

However, if you are willing to be a part, a small part, of a growing **CHURCH in the city**, a call is no more necessary than it is to join any other church. In fact a "Call" can be highly deceptive. Few calls come with a timeline. Many calls get misinterpreted. Calls are not forever.

But the Bride of Christ is indeed forever. So come enjoy the fellowship with fervent Believers who are different from you. No law against it.

MYTH 2: You Need a Program

From my current point of view, much of what passes for "city ministry" is simply a structured way for outsiders to feel comfortable (and rewarded) for small amounts of time spent doing things **TO people** who happen to reside in the city and seem "different." The very easiest way to minister or be ministered to, is simply to go talk to city people and build a relationship with them!

But we don't do that.. First we have to find all the negative statistics we can to justify our response to a **"Need."** "We must go to the most crime-ridden, HIV positive, most school drop-outs, least "Christian," most needy, etc." Somehow in our "ministry mind" we must identify the "problems" with others and rush to present our solution.

Why should a program and a need be necessary for us to come out of our comfort zone a few hours a month and worship with people who know God in a way that we don't...and perhaps never will?

Instead, a program must be identified that will respond to our determinations. If we can't see the program from the suburbs, perhaps one must be created, usually with a Non-profit Corporation filing to raise funds to pay for a program that is not particularly proven.

Is that necessary?

I once took a couple of my urban friends, part of our gang, **the Duce Posse**, to a suburban church Sunday service that featured a "Pepper and Salt" preaching duo of one black man and one white man. As a part of the conclusion they called people who were interested in the city and it's needs to attend a second meeting immediately after the first. Since the main service had over a thousand in attendance, I was quite surprised that less than 100 people attended the second gathering. They had just responded to an invitation at a larger meeting to "get more involved in the city." After some blather from the front, guided by one of the junior pastors over some abstract possibilities, I was nudged sharply by my gang to respond. I stood up, explained who we were and invited them to a simple **"Come on Down"** and hang out in **the "hood."** We gave out an address and phone number, come as you are, whenever you can. (The urban poor don't take vacations, don't venture far from their dwellings, don't pay a lot of attention to day or night nor do they carry calendars, so anytime is just fine.) Exactly 2 of the suburban folk came… once. They seemed to have a good time, but it didn't fit their expectations. Their view of how the city folk lived just wasn't true, which was rather bewildering.

I concluded that such an invitation is simply too terrifying and disorganized to suit the majority mind, so complex organization is necessary both mentally and structurally to help the fearful suburban folk deal with this. I have tried a variety of ways to communicate this to white folks over the years, but without much more than the occasional success.

I now have a simple mantra that I will repeat the rest of my days as a solution: *"Go to your early service in your regular church and then go to a black church one Sunday a month…for the next 10 years!"*

I have a list of churches in Baltimore that would be happy to have these visitors, but there have been few takers and even fewer a second time!!! Yes, it is a bit like taking a drink of water from a fire hose, but each Sunday it gets a little easier. But fearing the simple ways, we must now turn to the complex and convoluted with accompanying pitfalls.

And, of course, the **existing program of God for reaching the city is the black church,** more on that later, but let's deal with some other realities first.

MYTH 3: The Myth of the Virtuous Truly Needy

One of my first, "doing things the hard way" plan involved rental property in the poorest of neighborhoods. I was a landlord for 10 years; "Decent Housing at a Fair Price" was my goal. One of the things I learned early in the game was that there were reasons the poor were poor. They made bad decisions (as if I never did!). I would look at a woman with 4 or 5 kids, all with different fathers, none of whom were around, and I would have loved to say, **"Have you heard of birth control?"** I watched the way they spent money and I wondered, **"Can any of you do math?"** I heard them curse at their children, call them names and yell at them. I wanted to say, **"Can you encourage your kids instead of putting them down?"** I watched one family and noted that if a choice could be made between a right decision and a wrong one, they chose the wrong one EVERY TIME! Bad parenting was followed generationally by worse parenting. Poor judgment was followed by more poor judgment. I could not deny they had needs, I could also not deny that they were simply self-destructive people. Initially I thought they were just stupid, but that wasn't true…they could be clever as foxes. I found that there was no "pure" needy, most of them were contaminated by factors I didn't understand. I found that the more I knew, the less I knew. But I kept trying to learn. It was a little like trying to fix a bad car. Nothing stayed fixed, and more stuff broke. My favorite bumper sticker was, *"The difference between genius and stupidity is that genius has its limits!"*

I suspect that many people have a model in their mind of what the poor should be like. And how they should respond to the help we offer. Those of us who are around the poor for years, have no model, but we have many stories! Thankfully, I am not stuck in that rut anymore, **I was the one who changed, not the poor**! As it turned out, the obvious was not the real cause, I was mostly seeing the effects.

By the way, let me "call out" a connected myth, **that Home Ownership Creates Virtue.** I am about to discuss programs to connect with the poor, including housing, but I want to raise an eyebrow over the unreasonable expectations associated with home ownership. Some people think that Habitat for Humanity and their plan to make homeowners in the city, is the key to reconstructing the city. It isn't.

First, it is on too small a scale. There are at least two Habitats functioning in Baltimore, but even combined, they only rehab a couple handfuls a year. Second, as an unwanted side effect, they tend to trap people in neighborhoods. While they claim to "not charge interest" on the resulting loans on the homes, they often do sell the mortgages at a discount to financial institutions, who, in effect, do collect interest. But the recipients/buyers cannot sell a $130,000 house, which is what it cost to rehab, with a $100,000 mortgage in a $50,000 neighborhood. The only way they can move is to walk away. And that does happen. I am not saying it is a bad program, I am saying that most people expect too much from it. It must be part of a larger connection to a neighborhood and church.

The unwanted side effect is that it traps people in struggling neighborhoods. Often the people who tend to support Habitat look to build those houses in neighborhoods that are not their own!

MYTH 4: The Myth of "Need," That the Poor Need Stuff (More Than a Relationship).

There may be more than one kind of house that people suggest for the poor!

GINGERBREAD HOUSE

"We want to do something nice for the poor for Christmas." Caught a bit off guard, I hesitated. A group of three or four college students huddled around me and further asked, "Do you know some poor people?" I did indeed.

"What do you want to do?" I asked, rather puzzled over the possibilities. "We loved Gingerbread Houses when we were growing up, so we wanted our small group to make some as a project and give them to needy people for Christmas," they said.

I agreed to supply the needed contacts with poor people, but was a bit taken back. The culture gap between college students at a very prestigious Eastern university and urban African American poor was rather substantial. As it turned out, it was a challenge on my part to find suitable economically challenged recipients.

Then I thought of Lottie and Richard. Lottie had reached the age milestone where she wanted to work, but could no longer do so. Her Social Security was minimal. Richard was there as well, but despite having the most arthritis-deformed feet and ankles I have ever seen, he still tried to make a few bucks on good days. When he could, he worked a couple blocks away with a group of street mechanics. You could get simple mechanical jobs, like brake pad replacement, new radiators, water pumps, universal joints and the like done next to the curb…while you waited and cheaply. It is part of the unseen urban industry, a service for those with limited funds who needed to keep their cars maintained so they could get to work. Richard was well known and liked, to mention his name to that mechanic crew was to get special treatment from them. But I shudder to think how painful it was for him to work.

The day came when the students were to present their very nicely done Gingerbread House to Lottie and Richard. I had tried to prepare them to receive it as well as the students to give it. But I was not up to the task. It was a bit clumsy as Lottie and Richard were not sure what to do with the house. The students were a bit overwhelmed with the situation and at a loss for words. I explained that it was ok to EAT the house, which brought a look of horror to Lottie's face, since it was a very nice house. The gingerbread was well assembled and the decorations were perfect. The students nodded and smiled, affirming my barbaric suggestion. They stared at each other a bit and then Lottie grabbed each of them and gave them her best bear hug! That should have bridged the gap, but it overwhelmed the quiet students even more! Their eyes widened and a look of panic was on their faces!

We made our retreat; I think all of us were relieved after this encounter. Lottie and Richard thanked me again later for the Gingerbread House, but made no mention of what they did with it! They were touched by the student's desire to care for them, but were at a bit of a loss in responding. The students never mentioned it again. I suspect the whole experience, with the sights, smells, and people that were so different from them, was simply too much. The communication gap was a large one, the experience gap an even bigger one.

From that difficult experience, I became determined to narrow the gap of understanding as much as I could when introducing people who were different. I work now through churches and with people who are prepared to reach out to students who are easily overwhelmed by urban life. I learned that if people's perceptions are overwhelmed by an experience, they simply cannot see, hear or take in additional information.

What the students missed, thanks in part to my blunder, was the opportunity to enjoy Lottie and Richard. They both knew Jesus, perhaps in different ways than the students understood. But that fellowship didn't happen. It should have. So, I am committed to doing better.

Oh, and no more gingerbread houses.

So What Can We Do?

Traditionally, the city has been viewed as a "needy place," so most of the initial efforts to minister in the city have focused on **observed NEED as a comparison to the USA middle class**. If we compare our urban poor to the rest of the world, we have very rich poor!

I think it is worthwhile to divide the usual efforts into two general categories. They will gain greater significance later in this book. Those categories are *giveaways* and *interactives*.

There can be an underlying expectation. It is not necessarily wrong, but it is not always helpful. Like the "Carrot and Horse" metaphor, it can be hoped that by offering something, a certain behavior will be achieved. In exchange for a "giveaway," perhaps there will be church attendance. If the local rescue mission offers food and lodging, however meager, they expect to preach to the recipients. I have a long time friend who needed a place to eat and sleep a couple winters back, so he became a regular at a Mission. Having to listen to people who assumed their right to lecture the poor night after night so that he could sleep where it was warm, was not a pleasant experience! It takes a bit of the edge off the "salvation" reports.

Again, I am not condemning either giveaways or interactives, but I do want to deal with reality. In my opinion, the deciding factor is relationships. **It is the human contact that respects the needy AND RELATES TO THEM WITHOUT CONDESCENSION that is the important factor.**

Giveaways have involved but are not limited to:

1) **"Feeding"** the poor (the term reminds me of feeding the farm animals when I was growing up). Perhaps it is better to consider what Isaiah says, "Is it not to *share our bread with the hungry?* We don't quite do this. We share some of our *discretionary* funds in the form of a donation and some may spend time as a server for an organized meal. It is the first move toward the poor that people tend to make, along with donating to panhandlers, however.

2) **Clothing** the poor… with our old clothes, not so much taking them to the store…

3) Offering a variety of **medical assistance**. Think Good Samaritan Hospital. The name of a city hospital in Baltimore. I like Bon Secours, also.

4) **Employment assistance**. Usually takes the form of "Job Counseling," a very difficult and thankless task. Helping the unemployable find jobs is for the true saints. I managed property for Jubilee Baltimore, which also housed Jubilee Jobs. There was a steady stream of needy people looking for work that passed through. Many found jobs but both discovering the job openings and getting applicants prepared was VERY difficult. There was a true Saint who worked there, Olga Saunders. She was a grandmother who spent every day trying to get some of the most difficult people employment.

5) **Eviction prevention**. Usually a small check written to the landlord, normally prolonging the eviction process, not eliminating it. Those who struggle with rent payments rarely overcome their lack of finances and lack of cash management skills.

6) **Education assistance** … After school programs, tutoring programs and GED programs

7) Several types of **advocacy**…Legal, Justice issues, potentially favorable lawmaking for the poor.

In general, the poor are assumed to want these services but the poor are rarely given **the power to instigate or terminate** the services. In fact, it is not uncommon for them to resent "free" services, but they know not to bite the hand that feeds them. Often that "hand" also treats them like animals and wastes their time. But they don't feel they can say anything about that.

Interactives represent a little more impact, tho over a longer period. They may still be controlled by the donors but are more user friendly. **They can be done WITH people instead of just "For" them or "To" them**. That includes but is not limited to:

1) All types of housing efforts; rentals, development and rehabs

2) Community development, the enhancement of community desirability and resources

3) Community organization, the empowering of a group of citizens

4) Job training, job development, job creation

5) "Homecoming," assisting the return of those incarcerated

6) Food coops,

7) Community gardens

8) AIDS related services, including group type homes and care.

Again, I don't mean to criticize those who do their best to serve in either **a giveaway or interactive** effort. When you look from a needs-based perspective, the natural response is to do something about it. Those on the receiving end certainly appreciate it. But it may not be the only part of the equation. Not only that, it may be the least effective; witness our last 50 years of a "War on Poverty."

Where are the relationships that last over time? That is the real need. Can we be "WITH" them instead of doing things "FOR" them or "TO" them?

A hard thing is to define exactly WHAT is expected from the efforts expended on EITHER giveaways or interactives. Frequently the real expectations differ greatly between the donors and the recipients. Additionally, there always seems to be an uncomfortable distance between donor and recipient.

By the way, that was one of Ola Saunder's secrets. She was the heart and soul of **Jubilee Jobs**. She was involved in her client's whole life! Day after day there were people lined up to be encouraged and to report to Ola. Sooner or later everyone seemed to find a job.

When carefully combined with the efforts of a church or local group, interactives can be quite a life-saver and a witness. WITHOUT that local, personal connection, the real effect on people may be quite limited.

Do you have secret hopes that your city contribution will change lives? What if it doesn't?

MYTH 5: Black and White People Can and Should Work In "Partnership"

First a story: A group of elephants liked to dance and liked to watch the reality dance programs on television. They noticed that a couple groups of mice across town were gifted dancers, but lacked the promotional resources to get noticed by the TV folks. They decided that partnership would further the desires of both groups, so they approached the mice. At first everyone was nice and their mutual admiration for dance was a common ground. But then the wise old head mouse gently suggested that a dance group of elephants and mice was not quite a simple as it might seem. For one thing, a mouse dancing with an elephant had more on their mind than just their own footwork. A mouse stepping on an elephant's toe would hardly be noticed, while if the elephant stepped on the mouse it could be fatal!! As the relationship progressed, other differences were noticed. Since elephant feet are not that flexible and elephant tails not particularly controllable, mice were able to do things with their feet and tails that elephants simply did not notice or appreciate. Conversely, since mice did not possess a trunk, they had no appreciation for the stylish movements a trunk could make. But rather than reject the whole notion, which had been done before, they decided that if the elephants could offer some resources, attend mouse dance contests, learn to appreciate fine movement and cheer loudly (the mice could only squeak, not trumpet), the whole mouse-dance program could be celebrated. Of course, some of the elephants resented all the attention being given to the mice. They resented that their money was being spent by the mice and none of it came back to them. But the elephants who became more aware of how the mouse-dance culture worked, gained a new appreciation for ways to make the elephant-dance program something more than just a grass-smasher and a zombie apocalypse for the mice.

Yes, the obvious parallel is between a small black church and a larger suburban church. Perhaps an equal partnership cannot be achieved. But does it even need to?

In my opinion, there is no need for partnerships — only servant relationships! Black church leaders are in fact leaders, so let them lead. White folks can just follow...problem solved!

About 25 years ago, the decision was made to close Campfield Elementary School, near where I live and where my three children were going to school. We had meetings with the school board and the usual hearings, but there was a cultural "fact" that drove the decision. **"You can bus black kids to a white school, but you cannot bus white kids to a black school."** When I testified before the County School Board, I begged them to not close our school based on this reason. I was ignored. Could it be that you can **"get black people to attend a white church, but you cannot get white people to attend a black church?"** *(perhaps for much the same reason as the school busing claim)* Is that possible?

Returning to the story, Yes, the white church is the elephant and the black church the mouse. Attempts have been made many times to have a partnership between black and white churches, but they seem to be like an elephant dancing with a mouse. The mouse has a lot to lose and the elephant doesn't understand that. People who are fans of "Partnerships" have a hard time believing it won't work very well. Still others believe that the black folks should simply come to a white church, or that whites have little or nothing to gain from attending a black church.

Beware of a hidden CONTROL REVERSAL

In the world of aviation, few things are more dreaded than "control reversal." What it means is that under some circumstances, the flight controls abruptly do the opposite from what is expected. We had a crash at my favorite grass-strip airport, "Green Landings," a couple years ago, because someone hooked up the control cables backwards! When the wing dropped on one side, the control corrections made it worse and the plane ended up in the trees! In the world of the poor, **if what you give them or do for them has the opposite effect, it is the equivalent of a control reversal.** Corbett and Fikkert do an excellent job of outlining some of this in their book, "When Helping Hurts." Part of what I am suggesting is that in many cases, the instinctive helping that people offer has an opposite or negative effect down the road. Not infrequently, that result is not noticed because a program may be so firmly entrenched that no one wants to cancel it or the originators have long since moved on and don't want to hear about it. We are hoping to be a bit wiser as we think about all this. Suppose we start at a different point.

Focusing on Assets...a Secret Theme?

What is usually overlooked is the assets and skills that are possessed by a community and individuals in that community. Rural families tend to train their children to learn, work and have faith within a known, existing system. Not so much African American inner-city single moms. Those children are trained to be survivalists (see myth #1, next chapter). They are highly skilled at "feeling" what is happening on their street, responding to threats, and getting what they want. They have often learned that authority figures, like their parents, police, school teachers and employers are not to be trusted because they have **only their own interests at heart**. But of what use is an asset if no one recognizes it? If the real asset is people but if cultural blindness is at work, then what? Perhaps we need to look again to see those assets. And how they are utilized. Do you really think a parachurch group from the suburbs is more likely to assist those assets than a local church with empowered indigenous people?

MYTH 6: The City Can BE FIXED!!

I suspect that is the secret desire all of us bring to the city, that there are simple, lasting solutions to all the city problems. If you read books like Taylor Field's, "Graffiti Church," you can see the thoughts of others, at least indirectly, in hoping, "JESUS IS THE ANSWER." This may be the point your theology runs over a rock. If I say, **"Jesus ISN'T the answer, nor are you,"** does that kind of chafe your convictions? What I am suggesting is the mere mention of Jesus isn't enough. It takes some soldiering. The strongholds of Satan are indeed strong. What if **City people don't lack information, they lack example and encouragement**?

Here is the key reality word to remember. **RELENTLESS.** The City culture is RELENTLESS. It never sleeps, it never quits, and it is open 24/7. The worker who gets involved in the life of the urban poor has a limited energy span, but the street world is not so limited.

I mention Ralph, my very long term urban friend. His life experience as well as medical conditions make him a chronic (not curable) person, not an acute (short term recoverable) one. The next phone call from him is likely to bring a chronic problem not an acute joy. While he is clean of illicit drugs, he needs prescribed meds to deal with chronic back pain (opiates!) and meds to deal with schizophrenia and bipolar disorder. His disorganization is likely to lead to some kind of overdose or under dose...while living in a hostile environment. And I am his father-figure now that he is in a manic phase. His chronic struggles have become my chronic struggles.

There is a reason most people move away from the toxic part of the city. They can't stand it anymore. Yes, that just makes it worse, but at least they are not there to see it. Is that move justified? Maybe, maybe not.

I understand that some organizations are advocating "Re-Neighboring" and move-backs to the city, but anyone doing so must be prepared for chronic people. There is a reason most black pastors don't live in the neighborhood anymore and that the parsonages next to the churches are vacant. They can never escape the **relentless** street life.

There are some groups that have been formed to "transform" the city. To change what is existing. But they are usually rather vague and short on specifics when asked "Change into What?" Change into the Suburbs? Who says the suburbs are without sin?

What if it were about changing relationships, one person at a time?

CHAPTER 4

4 MYTHS ABOUT RACE AND RACISM

As I write this, I am observing the USA moving into the next phase of "peeling the Racism onion." Police Departments are under scrutiny for skin-color based unequal treatments. The statues dedicated to Civil War heroes on the Confederate side are being removed. "White Supremacists" are being called out and their public demonstrations challenged. But much is still secret.

MYTH 1: Everyone has the same opportunity.

The myth begins with an assumption that everyone wanted to be in the USA. However, being captured and sold into slavery of the most horrifying kind **is not that**. The heritage of most black folk is being part of that lineage. Hostages. Chattel. Cruelty. Rape. Murder and Lynching's. Being "documented" but being of slave lineage is light years different than all other immigrants! If your DOCUMENTATION IS A BILL OF SALE, what are you supposed to do with that? Lumping them together is not a matter of justice but rather convenience.

Equal Opportunity to Grow Up?

Usually once a week or so I see my grandkids. They all have two parents, a nice house, a secure neighborhood, opportunity to learn and thrive, food, guidelines, only encouragement…no ridicule, a warm place to sleep and no financial fears. A grandmother cares for them two days a week while their mother works, and the TV is NOT on. Generally, they are allowed a little TV each day, the rest of the time they get to work and play.

I see kids who are the same age in the city and the "script flips." One parent, crummy house, dramatic neighborhood, no books in the house, no playground, intermittent food, no separate education and the TV is on 24-7. Not every household in the city, of course, but in far too many.

The contrast could not be any more dramatic. Two sets of kids, about 8 miles apart, but hugely different childhoods. No way on God's Green Earth do they both have equal opportunity! As to be expected, that disparity has a profound effect, *sooo deep* that few outside the inner city have much comprehension of the impact.

I want to address that indirectly by offering a lens to look through.

Survivalist vs. Intentionalist

Growing up in Iowa on a farm, I learned that by setting goals, learning, working hard and persevering, I could get what I wanted. I became a licensed pilot, licensed commercial driver, licensed plumber, licensed real estate salesmen, college grad, Army Officer, jack of all trades, campus minister, middle manager, Sub-S Corporation owner, etc. I took full advantage of being a member of the majority race, solid family values, conservative politics and good financial planning. I am a full blown **INTENTIONALIST!** I set and accomplished goals that took decades to bear fruit, but that fruit showed up. I am retired with no mortgage, significant, retirement investments, but mostly living on combined Social Security benefits by keeping overheads low. A comfortable enjoyable life.

Contrast that with my friend Ralph. His long-term "wife" struggles to find work and overcome depression, His parents were not living together growing up, his mother had several children, limited education and limited resources. He grew up in inner city Baltimore and has no licenses, just a General Education Diploma (GED), earned only recently. He fathered children at an early age, had difficulty obtaining and maintaining employment, and began to self-treat schizophrenia and bipolar disorder with street-available drugs. He missed being a paraplegic by one inch from a stabbing in prison. He does possess skills, however. He is a **SURVIVALIST** of the highest order. He can survive on the streets, survive in prison without joining the gangs, respond instinctively and instantly to the actions of others on the streets. He is the master of the moment, being able to obtain food, shelter and relationships where there seem to be none. He remembers people, places and things. He doesn't forget a face or where he saw it. "See that dude? He was in Hagerstown (a state prison) and hangs on Eager Street." He has learned that it is useless to plan much beyond tomorrow. Given that 1 in 8 black men in Baltimore will be shot sometime in their life, he doesn't plan very much. Oh, he has dreams, but not all that realistic. He is an Urban Expert, a quiet shadow in the room, but a skilled observer in any setting. He is respected on his street by "Killer," the young gang leader as well as many others.

The Survivalist has learned to be **reactive** more that proactive or even interactive. They can read the minds of the Intentionalist as it pertains to them. For example, a panhandler or beggar, the obvious survivalists in the city, MUST know who they are engaging and what line to use…if they want to survive. The converse is not true. Intentionalists are lousy at understanding the world of the survivalist, particularly if race is involved. At the heart of it is the truth that **THEY DON'T HAVE TO!** Since Intentionalists control the world, they do not NEED to understand the Survivalist world…and they usually don't. They assume that since they define reality, there cannot be another one. Having spent some 30 years in the urban world of Survivalists, I find it more complex than ever. So beware of the person with lots of simple answers and a strong desire to "change the city." They probably don't "get" it.

One lesson to be learned from the Survivalist is to live in the "NOW." To be present **now**. Many Intentionalists live for what they plan to do in the future, **missing today while dreaming about next week**.

I need to add one more category. **The Irrational**. Of course, they exist in most groups and classes, but cities are a haven for people who think differently. One can be a misfit in other situations, but be operational and survive in the City. One of the reasons it takes time to connect with people in the city is the high level of Irrationals around. They can be easier to spot with some of the homeless or outspoken urban poor, but I also know an attorney who was in effect a con man before he was disbarred, and I also know some pastors who live in a dream world of lies and deceit. This becomes more difficult with greater interaction. I had a discussion with a man at church recently who was fully convinced he was being treated like a chump because he was asked to do work beyond his job description as a porter. I explained that he was being paid for his time; therefore the job was irrelevant, from his employer's perspective, but he walked off in a huff. It was about respect for him vs. power for his employers. The likely outcome is his dismissal from the job because he will have a hard time understanding the other point of view, which is backed by authority. Since he has spent most his life in prison, these concepts come hard for him. Do I have a suggestion? Yes, let God give understanding. Rationality does not translate well to the irrational; understanding must come to them on their wavelength. Yelling does not work as a means!!

Instead, it can be a mental dysfunction or simple non-linear thinking. For example, it can be instructive to listen to those who have opposite political views. The thoughtful person will note that each has a predisposition to a view that is easily countered by the observable facts. Not a problem for city dwellers. "Rabid" sports fans are a good example. They may dress everyday with their favorite team jersey and no one thinks twice. In the same way, an introverted accountant can put on leather clothes, a helmet and throw his leg over a Harley Davidson motorcycle and be a Poser!

The irrational may be found in both the ranks of the survivalists and the ranks of the intentionalists. They may also be other "missioners" who are determined to do things their way. But many of us come from a rational world or at least it seems so to us. But trying to make the irrational into rational is a job by itself. It may be mental illness, it may be personality type, and it may defy definition. The main thing is to not be surprised when conflicts occur. This shows up when people have conflicts over minor things but make them a capital offense. A lack of respect can result in a murder, for example. More on dignity and respect later.

MYTH 2: All Minorities Are Created Equal and Should Be Treated as Such.

It has been common practice for white organizations to lump any people of color together and treat them as "minorities." By default, it also causes the designated minorities to compete for the attention of the parent organization. All this in the name of "equality," of course. Let's think about this. Were all minorities subjected to racism…yes, but in varying type and degree. Were all minorities slaves at some point, kidnapped and locked into slavery? **Um, no.** Are the real expectations different from one group to another? **Oh, Yeah.** Does that matter? **Absolutely.**

Let's think about this for a moment. Let's try and get some use out of that old broken tool, the **Stereotype.** For the following groups, what is their highest cultural value? Again, **think stereotypes.**

Asians How about **education?**

Hispanics How about **contribution?**

African Americans How about **dignity and respect?**

Caucasians How about **power and control?** (Power is used here as simply a broad term for the ability to get something done and/or knowing people who can get something done)

I need to point out at this juncture that nearly all my experience is with AA folks and somewhat with Korean culture. But it is rather thin when it comes to all Asians and even thinner with Spanish-speakers. But precisely because I have spent the last 30 years and more trying to understand and become a cultural insider to the black folk in the USA, I claim that they are not like other people of color.

I watched an interaction with an Italian American foreman and an African American laborer. "Go get the red flag and be a flagman." Said the Foreman. "I don't do flagman" said the laborer, who was shoveling gravel at the time. "Do what I say," said the foreman, "or just hit the road." The laborer just walked away from the job and never came back. In the mind of the laborer, he was above being a flagman. In the mind of the foreman, a laborer was, well, a laborer.

Think about this: Is there a conflict between having a high cultural value for **power and control** and a high cultural value for **dignity and respect**? Absolutely, it can be a train wreck! People of power tend to place the respect of persons second to getting a job done (there is another story coming along about this). People of respect tend to make work subservient to respect. In simple terms, the cultures clash at the highest levels. Yes, individuals alter that because they may have adopted different views. But one need only to look at the unemployment levels for each cultural group to notice the black folk, particularly hourly workers, have a tougher time staying employed in a white world. And a major part of that is simply different values. And being VALUED!

My daughter worked as a Registered Nurse for a couple years in the government hospital at Shiprock, NM, that catered almost exclusively to the Navajo people. She found that building relationships was very difficult with people who lived on the reservation. The Navajo children would simply stare at her when they got their immunization shots, the Caucasian children would scream like she had just cut off their arm! Her supervisor, a Navajo, said with a chuckle, "Navajos don't even like each other very well, that's why we live far apart. So don't expect to build much of a relationship as a white person!" When I visited her, despite my years in cross-cultural connecting, I found it very difficult to feel where people were coming from. Even though the AA in Baltimore and the Navajo in New Mexico are considered minorities, they have virtually nothing in common when it comes to culture. As a landlord, I had one of the concentrations of Lumbee Indians (their term) on the East coast living in my apartments. They had intermarried with AA folks and are very much urban dwellers...but they are the exception. In places where assimilation could occur, it has, but as is the base culture between urban and rural, AA and NA folks can be very different.

I submit that any USA organization must treat minorities DIFFERENTLY from each other but with EQUALITY for all. Since the values and experiences are so vastly different, CONFLICT is to be expected and will need to be embraced in a variety of ways. Lumping everyone into a "minority" category simply forces them to compete with each other and with whites. Not fun for them.

MYTH 3: Racism Has About Finished Its Course.

A significant book for me recently has been "White Trash. The 400-year Untold History of Class in America" by Nancy Isenberg. By the way, this is the most heavily researched book I think I have ever discovered. It is very compelling to consider how this country has always been classist. Simply put, they emptied out the alleys, gutters, back streets and brothels of Western Europe, particularly England, and shipped the white trash to America. Then the aristocracy went out and bought slaves when tobacco and cotton became a gold mine. The white trash were appeased by the aristocrats telling them that the worst of their lot was better than the best black man......and so the battle has raged.

It has always been about land, material goods and money. Racism by the color of one's skin was a matter of convenience and concession. The sole right to vote was held by the male landed gentry for more than 100 years, except for the Native Americans. They became citizens in 1925, They had to wait for their right to vote until 1957!

So we have always been a society in denial about class. But we all know who is above us and below us if we are honest about it. The higher your class, the greater your right to sit in judgment, criticize and analyze others. And that right is never questioned.

If you were born after 1995 or so, your perspective on race and racism is likely to be different than us old folks. You may think that with the Obama Presidency and other events, that things are nothing like the days of Rev. Dr. Martin Luther King, Jr. And to some extent, you will be right. But the further you go into the city, you may discover that the core of race issues in the USA is still alive and well. 75% of white people in the USA have no black friends. Iowa, where I grew up, is still more than 90% white, even though it was 98% white when I grew up. More troubling is that it may be harder for you to be motivated to real understanding… because of Polyculturalism (a simple acceptance of all cultures). But I want to encourage you to **consider White Privilege, Social Capital, Paternalism, bias, discrimination, hypersegregation** and other parts of racism which have effectively separated people. And then how to bridge **that gap in your understanding**. Why? Because a part of God is out there to bless that understanding.

From my observation, **white folk seem to be** *scared*! Hardly a week goes by but some prominent white person gets caught making a racist statement. So, most whites will go to great lengths to avoid anything that might get them in trouble. When someone tells me a race joke, if as a white man in the USA I will appreciate the put-down of a minority, they lower their voice and look around as if we are Cold War spies! This tends to happen in my age group, since we were the ones who were openly taught racism in all phases of our culture. Again, I grew up in a world that was 98% white people, so we mostly noted class distinctions between whites. I had developed a sense that would let me know instantly what class a person was if I could see them get out of their vehicle and walk down the street. There was a class hierarchy based on what vehicle was driven, the clothes they wore and the confidence displayed in their walk. I realized when I moved into a black majority world that I could develop the same skills if I worked at it. With perception and thought, I could instinctively know what to say in greeting by "feeling" who they are. I still work at it all the time. And it pays off.

IN THE ELEVATOR

I got on the elevator at the 5th floor of the parking garage at the Casino/Mall and was suddenly joined by about 10 assorted African Americans, who quietly filed in after me. The last one squeezed in, facing the group, as the doors closed behind him. He glanced at me and within a millisecond I smiled and slightly nodded.

You see, in that instant, I instinctively knew he was a natural wit, a master of the word spoken in jest, a very funny man. I was not disappointed. "Gonna get rich today!" he wisecracked and was rewarded with an uproar of laughter. The audience participated with jest and banter as well, as if we had the briefest of church services. He had transformed an entire elevator car into his personal happy zone!

I was touched that he glanced at me first, to see if I was all right. I was encouraged that I responded and was then rewarded with a fantastic 20 seconds of experience with total strangers. I know in my heart that if I had given him a cold stare or looked away, he would have felt restricted and perhaps not even commented. But I joined the uproar, with gratitude.

And then we were on the first floor. We hushed immediately as though nothing had happened. We put our serious faces back on as the door opened and we all walked out. A brief encounter, to be sure. But it lasted a long time for me. It was the reward for many years of working to "tune in" to the culture of urban/suburban black people. Because in that instant and the following 20 seconds, I belonged. I was just a normal person who appreciated those around me. It's worse than that… It was no put-on, I felt at home. I had just visited a particular racial experience …and no one knew.

I am often asked by other white folks, "What makes you want to learn city culture, to live around black people?" For a while I responded, "It is the best kept secret in the world, to live in a middle-class black neighborhood" Having been in one for 34 years, I can't imagine living anywhere else.

Sometimes I tell the elevator story and ask, "What if we really don't know how black people enjoy life when we whites are not around? What if they have a really great experience and understanding that whites do not?" Then I note that it is hard to tell if the refrigerator light goes off when you close the door…unless you are IN the fridge!

But more than that, suppose that God has done something we whites have not accounted for…that he has indeed made the poor and downtrodden

RICH IN FAITH? What if there are riches to be found in black church that happens when we whites are not around? I am convinced that is true. Having been a strong part of a black church for many years now (16 years) I have to say that God met me there at every service I have attended. That has not always been the case in white church. I keep finding out things about God that I never imagined. You see, the Holy Ghost shows up! Don't miss it next time!

Better than???

Growing up I learned very early, though, that the "colored" were not like us. My grandmother had a statue of a young black child who was dressed up but was holding a fishing pole with a string that dangled in the water of the large bird bath. "Lawn jockeys" were very popular back in the day and no one (at least in Iowa) thought them offensive. I remember as a child thinking black kids must be stupid to fish in a bird bath!! Today, I have a black friend of prominence in Baltimore who has a collection of the very offensive postcards, china, and statues that white folk made. It is a very un-nerving house to be in if you are white! Interestingly, the National Football League Hall of Famer and Minnesota State Supreme Court Justice Allan Page also has a collection of racist memorabilia. That is unnerving also!

My children grew up in a middle-class black neighborhood and went to mixed or predominately black schools. They don't think of race jokes unless it is to remark about the lack of intelligence on the part of those who tell them. Their friends are of mixed ethnicity and they are more polycultural. My son called me the other day and said, "Dad, don't you get tired of racist white people and their complaining?" Yes, I do.

I was working on a house in the "Pigtown" area of Baltimore which is mostly hard-living whites a few years back when a white passer-by struck up a conversation. He quickly commented about how black people were driving the City of Baltimore down. So I asked him,

"When is the last time people from Africa tried to rule the World?" He had no answer.

"When is the last time people from Germany tried to rule the world? That he knew. "World War I and World War II"

"What is your heritage?" I asked. "German, " he replied. I responded with the same, my great-grandparents had emigrated in 1890's

"So aren't we more of a problem than black people? " I asked. "Black people are not the ones causing wars." Without a word, he turned and walked away.

Most white folk fail to recognize the two major operators and perpetrators of Racism in the USA... The first is WHITE PRIVILEGE.

In simple terms, **white privilege** means that because of the mechanism of society is set up to benefit white folk, they need not concern themselves with changing their life to accommodate minorities they care little about. They can ignore all kinds of people of color and nothing bad happens. They need not learn Spanish, eat kimchee, cook with rice, buy foreign cars, or change their circle of friends. Their children will be accommodated by colleges, fraternities, major employers, church, and people of power because the schools, churches and opportunities are geared to them. They know the system of how to get places, make money, store money, buy stuff, build an inheritance and structure their lives for "success." Much of the information is simply not shared with minorities. The presentation of a white face to a white institution invokes a solid point of understanding. The benefit of the doubt is likely to be extended as opposed to the benefit of the doubt being revoked, as in the case of dark-skinned people.

If I am stopped by the Police in Baltimore, and it is quite unlikely, I will be treated with respect. For about 6 years I had a Concealed Carry Permit and carried a gun as a landlord. On a couple occasions, my gun became un-concealed, but I was not questioned nor was my permit requested. I was even allowed to carry my pistol into the Courthouse once because I forgot to leave it in my truck. Some fast talking and I was allowed in the building after showing my permit. It did make their metal detector howl like a wolf! No way would a black person be treated like that.

The other term that is related is "**Social Capital.**" It is that **group of family, neighborhood, church, school, fraternity, and peers that connects the individual to opportunity**. That series of relationships is like money in the bank. The poor have little social capital, the rich usually got rich because they have lots of social capital. The down side is that many of the capital-rich believe that work and working hard trumps relationships and that the goal in life is to acquire and consume as much GOOD stuff as possible. Families teach their children about 401(k) accounts, investments, credit and net worth in a variety of ways. Inheritance always looms on the horizon, that old family member might be LOADED! "I had to work" will serve as an acceptable excuse for most whites to justify the non-presence at events, even important family ones.

A friend of mine Dr. Stephanie Boddie, contributed to a book that discusses "The Church as Social Capital." While the importance of a church connection may be dwindling somewhat, it is still an important part of the black community. Church is more than worship, it is the weekly point of connection to people of faith. But those are limited connections compared to white church and white Social Capital.

White folks can also be BLIND..and it costs them little! In my experience; it is difficult for the average white person to even see **White Privilege**. It only shows up to them in the presence of minorities. Even then, it may not be obvious to them. At a recent AFAM (African American) Navigator conference in Cleveland, I arrived early and requested an early room. The gracious middle-aged white woman who was managing the front desk of the hotel was anxious to accommodate me, an old but handsome devil! The black person with me (a senior member of the Navigators) was not offered an early room. When she saw that he was with me, she reluctantly found a room for him, at my request. The next day, another black friend was denied an early room, even though he was registered! A simple mix-up and misunderstanding? Perhaps, but when such events happen with some regularity, it builds a strong case for white privilege…that a **white face is a passport to favored treatment** or at least an exemption from unfavorable treatment. I find I am uncomfortable in the majority-white settings, because I fear the police will enforce petty laws and not give me a break. Interestingly, "favor" is something one prays for and thanks God for upon receiving it**…in black church frequently**, but seldom in white church, particularly middle class and above! Poor whites in poor churches are also likely to pray for "favor." So both may pray for what is denied by class and skin color.

Recently, one of the city guys I know was admitted to the psych ward of a city hospital. Staunch rules of privacy prevail these days and it is very difficult to even find out if they are present in the facility. But my white face and charm allowed me favor with the social workers, nurses and even the psych Doctor. My presence upped the level of care given to my man significantly, I firmly believe. I am not trying to fight that system but want to note that a black man with a white friend has an advantage in the city. My point is to **encourage more cross-cultural, cross-class friendships to create "favor"**.

One other major operator is **paternalism**. In simple form, it means that one person must "take care of" another based on the ethnicity and neediness of the minority. We all know about "Helicopter Parents" who hover over their children, texting, checking their locations by GPS , and phoning multiple times a day. The same kind of paternalism can be applied to minorities.

"**White man's burden**," was a term used in many circles. It simply meant that because the white man had created the problem of oppressed black people, he was bound to create a solution of his liking. In cities, housing projects were created out of a sense of paternalism to care for minority low-income persons. In effect, however, it "warehoused" the poor by isolating them from opportunities, and concentrated the negatives.

In Christian circles, contact with minorities seems to only come by "serving them." Remember my story about a church supporting only white initiatives? Very elaborate programs are set up every summer to connect the "haves" with the "have-nots" across the globe, also called "religious tourism."

Usually the persons that are a minority are not seen as equals to the white majority, but rather as "projects." Out of a "servant heart" things are done FOR or TO other people but not really WITH them because there is no real understanding of their culture. For that matter, the white folks really don't care all that deeply, as evidenced by their typical lack of preparation. This is where the "giveaway" program really shines. It is acceptable to spend a great deal of money to travel across the world to paint a building, run a Vacation Bible School, teach English classes, or serve in a soup kitchen, EVEN THOUGH just sending the equivalent money spent one the trip to the needy people would do more than the actual work performed, i.e. that money would have hired locals with greater skill and an effect on the economy. Also no one seems to think of building relationships for a lifetime with the people who are present. That, of course, is left up to the real "missionaries."

In the case of AA subculture in the USA, black and white churches may do a pastor-and-choir exchange or the like, but no white person plans to make that relationship last for the next 10 years or more. That would alter the notion of a superior position and cause the two people to be on equal footing, which is simply not done; or worse, **not even thought about.**

Remember our discussion about partnerships, the elephant and mouse? When I listen to the "short-term missions" trip, I never hear "I'm going back to see "Pablo" or "Aiesa." What I hear is that they are focused on going back to do another **job** that someone else could do. That makes me a bit sad.

MYTH 4: White People Can Self-Certify as "Not Racist."

I observe that a part of the psyche of the average white person in the USA today is self-certification. Because no racial discrimination or superiority is INTENDED, any such racist outcomes is simply not their fault. **I often hear a self-certification that begins, "I am not a racist, but..."**

I also heard that recently from a light-skinned Latino!

But isn't that a bit like a child throwing a forbidden ball in the house? The resulting destruction of pottery is not really excused by a desperate plea, "I didn't MEAN to, Mommy"! Woe to the person like myself who **points out "Paternalism" or "White Privilege" to another white person**, particularly if the offender considers themselves to be an upstanding Christian.

In a much earlier paper to my white church, I referred to some as "Fine Christian Racists." THAT didn't make them happy! The fear of being a racist comes out towards me in the form of denial, anger, or rationalization. None asked what my evidence was, they just strongly resented my implication! Most of the long-time activist people have tired of pointing out the hypocrisy that is part of being a white person in the

USA, unless their paycheck depends on it! Real humility as demonstrated by people with a heart and a desire to learn stands out quickly, even these days of "multiculturalism."

Institutional racism is simply the framework that has been installed to subtly make life better for white people. Their education institutions, including churches, help people move from school to work to investment to retirement. Because it doesn't consider the ethnicity of others (beyond a nod in the general direction of "multiculturalism"), it discriminates without trying to do so. If you are struggling with this notion, please Google "White Privilege" and do a bit more research.

It is institutional racism that prevents the self-certification. Unless white folks who grew up in the USA have done something to combat the racism/classism they were taught, **they are in fact, or in default, racists.** That is why white folk are afraid to open their mouths and be honest, even in Christian settings. In their heart they suspect they are what they fear, but hope that a proclamation to the contrary will save them. Perhaps not.

Putting it another way, as long as the system of class, white privilege, social capital and hyper segregation exist, white folks cannot self-certify. It is like having the shingles virus. You may not have any symptoms, but they could pop up anytime!

This is obvious by the presence **of HYPERSEGREGATION**. Right now, Baltimore is much more segregated in public schools than it ever was in the 1950's. Yet no white people take any responsibility for that negative action. In fact, whites are fighting any efforts to change school districts to alleviate the problem. Even lower class whites know it is a bad thing to have all black schools! Or so it would seem. In their hearts they don't want their kids to associate with black kids even at school! The same parents would likely self-certify they are not racist!

And then there is the **HYPERSEGREGATION on Sunday morning**. From being in real estate sales of church buildings, I visit a lot of churches. Very few of the black churches have more than one or two white faces in the congregation. Whites just don't want to attend. Conversely, white churches SAY they want minorities to attend, but make no attempt to make their church desirable to minorities. Even in something as small as the church color scheme. Black churches usually have color schemes that are warm and inviting. Not so much white churches. When it comes time to redecorate a church, they would never think of hiring a decorator that was a minority they are trying to attract. They paint their church to suit themselves. When you attend those churches, it is obvious. "This ain't your church." Yet the same people may have prayed for the "city" for years. Go figure.

Forensic Race Stuff

There are many ways people explain racism, but one of them is from a perspective of caste or class. The dumbest white man was superior to the smartest black man, or any other person of color for that matter. The race system told the white man so. As obvious discrimination has faded somewhat, that left some of the lower-class white folks without people "lower" than themselves, to their dismay. They could be out-ranked by some black people, so they resented the shift. One of my teachers of the nature of racism some years ago, a firebrand black woman named Mary, tried to point out that race was first about class. This is the United States of America, not "Downton Abby," how can that be?

I did work as a Service Tech on water heaters, particularly the large commercial ones, and had occasion to work in the high-rise offices of downtown Baltimore. I would carry my tool bag onto the elevator and go into the offices of top financial companies to fix their bathroom water heaters and the like.. I was directed on more than one occasion to "use the freight elevator," which was in the rear of the building. I wore whatever I wanted, since we were contracted, which might mean shorts and a golf shirt. I also carried a tool bag and a metal box/clipboard, so I didn't look my net worth. That also attracted some cold looks from all the folks wearing suits, particularly the secretaries and office managers. One time while on a service call I asked to see one of the fund managers for a major investment house, who happened to go to my church. They looked me over in horror, carefully questioned my intent and quickly told me he was 'out of town', which turned out to be true. Their eyes also told me to "get out!" For the upper classes, there are many defenses to keep the lower classes at bay, from secretaries, to service elevators, to gated communities, to private jets, to separate schools.

Historically, the Navigators started out as a lower-class effort, then proceeded upward. Today there is an outreach among the elite on Capitol Hill in Washington, D.C. and elsewhere. (It is done somewhat in secret, to protect the politics involved) Yet there is not enough discussion in the organization about how class works or its effects. Lower class folks are very in tune with it, however, and can read the prejudice very quickly. The pressure is to move upward, not downward in terms of relationships, housing and the accumulation of stuff. Garth Brooks' *I Got Friends in Lowly Places* is a good song but not a popular idea. Treating others as equals without being paternalistic is not easy. Hollywood glamorizes the cross-class love stories, but ignores the difficulties that class expectations present. They propose the crossing of class lines in a love story, but don't follow the couple into those years of marriage struggle with expectations and families. Interestingly, one-to-one ministry relationships have crossed class lines with some degree of success in the Christian world.

As a staff worker for both the Navigators and InterVarsity, I found it hard to make presentations to rich people. I was conscious of my Walmart-type clothes, farm background, limited income and frugal outlook. I often felt like a panhandler. Even the degree of success I had from doing the presentation was not enough to get me going to do others. Even now I frequently under dress to see how I will be treated. The pressures of class-consciousness are a force to be reckoned with. We often feel condescension on the lower levels of class that may not be intended by upper classes, but it is very real to us. So how do we see discipleship on the lower class levels in our society if we are Intentionalists?

Understanding class and all its ramifications is beyond the scope of this book, but here are a couple struggles.

1. Intentionalists and even some survivalists want **to move up in class**. Why? Life seems better for them. Like F. Scott Fitzgerald starts out in "the Great Gatsby," '**The rich are not like you and I…**', but we all want that experience. I occasionally play the Mega-Millions Lottery, (the retirement plan for the poor), and dream of what I would do with all that money. If I think about it hard enough and plan carefully, I am not so sure I want to win. A big lump of money will screw up all my relationships, with neighbors, friends, housing, toys, church, family and how I look at life. Realistically, it isn't worth it. But I still dream of moving up in class with potentially the same outcomes. Why? Because our culture celebrates upward mobility, we all wish to be that "slumdog millionaire."

2. For the last 30 years I have been **moving both up and down in class**, or at least that is my relational intention. I find there are unexpected rewards in my relationship with God, my outlook on life and a great improvement in thankfulness. I work to be comfortable and to make others comfortable in poverty surroundings. I don't have to have the best house in my neighborhood, even at worst it is "better" than my city friends' houses. I can take the time to 'smell the roses' because what is important isn't stuff…its people. I enjoy a vast selection of 'characters', men and women of distinct personality and traits. Mere 'stuff' isn't enough to get me recognized. I must be me and have the friends that I do. People must mean more than money.

3. We should NOT **expect minority college students to 'get religion' and aim to move downward in class to 'take care of their people'**. People in need are a part **of all** of us, not just those of matching skin pigment. A now-deceased friend, Rev. Elward Ellis, former Director of Black Campus Ministry for InterVarsity Christian Fellowship, talked about all the chicken dinners his black church sold to give him scholarships to college. He felt he owed it to them to do well and to lead as best he could. They were handling the needs of the poor, they wanted him to carry their investment to the rest of the world. No small expectation!! They did not want him to simply return to the neighborhood but wanted to live vicariously through his successes.

4. **Some of us can shrug** off the effects of class and are in cross-training to not only be multicultural but multiclass. I am friends with the President of a company owned by Berkshire Hathaway (Warren Buffet). If I text him anytime between 5 am and Midnight, I will get an answer back in 5 minutes, ANY day. How is that for commitment? Interestingly, If I text my buddy, Bishop James Adams, I will also get an immediate answer, probably by phone. For my city friends, I must go to where they are, they have no phone. Some relationships take more effort and cost more.

5. **Inheritance…** or lack thereof. As the recipient of my parents efforts to elevate their children though leaving an inheritance, it has made a significant difference. Yet that is not an option for many black families. Statistically they only hold 3% of the national wealth, despite being some 12% of the USA population. Worse, they cannot catch up in the current situation. They simply have no tradition of building wealth or keeping it. Or any training to that effect.

What About the Multi-Class, Multi-Cultural Church? Isn't That the Real Solution?

Many white folks think the solution is to have a church where **EVERYBODY has a place.** They KNOW they will feel better if they can look out over a congregation that has people of color, preferably several colors. Then they can feel better about racism. They can be multicultural, a real plus it would seem

First, most **"multicultural" churches, aren't**. More typically they are white-controlled but welcoming of others who are not mono-racial. The white folks love this concept, however, because at least they don't have to submit to a black pastor and a black congregation! Too harsh? Exactly what is stopping them from attending a black church now, other than their own fears and preference? I know of no Biblical rule that says "**Thou shalt have**

only one church that thou attendenths." The "single church" notion is driven by finances, I suspect. Most of us have some investment in multiple Christian groups.

Let me put it this way. Multicultural churches aren't the solution to racial separation, particularly in the city. I am not denying that a multi-skin color church is fun to attend and very welcoming. It just has little impact in the inner city, **BECAUSE THE BLACK CHURCH (AND HISPANIC) ALREADY KNOWS WHAT IT'S MEMBERS NEED!** I encourage the existence of multicultural churches, I am just claiming they are not a serious solution because they are not able to deal with the real issues city people face.

Unconvinced? OK, what language should the church use? Hispanics IDENTIFY with each other through Spanish. An English service has a very limited audience. Ditto for Korean, Japanese, Chinese, Laotian, etc. Think there will be a conflict of expectations, given the huge difference in primary cultural values? Good luck on finding a Pastor! He will need to speak at least 5 languages, have a very flexible theology, an incredible understanding of cultural nuances and be comfortable working with leadership communications difficulties. They are fun churches to attend, but not heaven to lead! Theology alone is a major struggle. Check the next 3 myths.

CHAPTER 5

THREE MYTHS FROM A LIMITED THEOLOGY

God is huge…beyond our comprehension. A friend shared one of his favorite quotes, "God created Man in his Image; we have been trying to return the favor ever since!" Somehow, we are always compelled to rewrite the Bible into Systematic Theology, think about God with Greco-Roman philosophy and pretend that God is not all about paradox. Out of that, we have ended up with a Gospel and Discipleship aimed at "Winners" and no so much for "Losers." Can we rethink that?

MYTH 1: The Myth of Narrow "Discipleship"

One size doesn't fit all. Having narrow expectations for the personal conduct of others is a formula for frustration.

Disciple making, as practiced and understood by many, is an intentional effort. We may even say **"intentional relationships" are the core we build on.** I learned in 1965 that if I spent enough time with a young-in-the-faith person of my race and class, I could impart goals, Bible and methods **that would result in my young disciple trying to disciple someone else in short order.** Among the white majority culture, I saw rapid growth and disciple making in college and military settings. Not so much when I began to reach out in the city.

At the heart of discipling efforts was Bible Study. Intentionalists learn to read, write and comprehend written materials at an early age, so that was an easy platform to begin using in campus and military, but not so easy for the survivalists. Theirs is a visual, vocal world. Much like the early days of Christianity, truth be told. For them, it was at least 4 decades, several lifetimes in those days, before any written words of what we consider to be the "New Testament" showed up in the form of passed-around letters. And over 1,000 years would pass until 1452 when Guttenberg perfected a movable-type printing press, which began the Bible and literacy we know today. So it is possible to make disciples **without being able to read the "Word"! But you must know the stories.**

Indeed, the first disciples were not Bible students, they were students of "Life with Jesus."

Returning to the Myth at hand, disciple making is not a myth. However, the way some Intentionalists tend to view it, they can **make it a myth when the same expectations are applied to the Survivalists**. Some dream that a city kid, like my friend "Killer" could become a Disciple and move up to being a major leader. Some might even suggest that to him. They overlook his lack of understanding of the middle-class world, let alone the upper class and his near-complete lack of tools to get there. He may, however, become a leader in his street world. In fact, he already is. He has a "crew."

Worse, they overlook a strong but usually unseen part of Racism called "**Social Capital**." You are reading this document because I happen to know some key people in the Navigators who encouraged me, a high school teacher who encouraged my writing, a college degree in English, and a desire to write. A street acquaintance named "Killer" lacks ALL social capital beyond his gang. NOTHING in his culture affirms him, he is, in fact, the Nihilist that Dr. Cornell West writes about in "Race Matters." He is not affirmed by anything in the USA culture for he is the proverbial "bad guy" in TV and movies, his relationships are usually transactional, and he HAS NO HOPE!!! I really mean he has no hope…without a relationship from someone WITH social capital and even then there are no guarantees. He has the words "Gods Family" tattooed on his chest (he is a 'Blood'), but I don't know of many churches that will be impressed when he takes his shirt off!

What I am condemning is offering **unrealistic hope**, particularly out of ignorance of a person's ASSETS. The young drug dealers I knew had dreams of buying new cars, buying big houses and of living the "thug life" in general. None of them had the slightest hope of attaining any of that. They were functionally illiterate, math challenged, drug addicted, socially hampered and poorly motivated. I didn't offer them blanket speculations of hope, I just helped them to accomplish what they saw as the next step. Those steps were not of my design but theirs.

MYTH 2: That God is Not in the City

Is the Black Church invisible or are people just keeping their eyes shut? **Could there be a more arrogant action taken by the predominately white church folk than the near total ignorance of the black church?**

This is manifested in multiple ways, but I want to focus on how it has played out in terms of city ministry.

When white folks are in their suburban churches, they don't see the black church in action. During the week, the white folks drive past black churches on their way to work but since they don't see people or efforts, they assume that nothing is happening; meantime nothing is happening in their white church during the day either!

I typically attend the "Watch Nite" or New Year's Eve service at Dynamic Deliverance Cathedral. It is over about 12:30 or 1 am. As I drive home, most churches are just letting out and there are committed Christian people everywhere on the Baltimore streets celebrating the New Year. The average white person would be home in bed and never see this. Instead, indignant over the "crime, degradation, joblessness and need," they assume that if something is to be done, they must do it. So the white churches form up and get tax exempt status for a variety of white-controlled efforts of Give-aways and Interactives. In Baltimore, I know of three ministries, some known nationally, that began with the white folks "parachuting" into a neighborhood and setting up shop. In all three cases, the white founders did not take the time to connect much with the existing black churches nearby. In one case, the white founder simply bought a whole church building, paid cash for it, and went into the evangelism business. They did all sorts of the giveaway programs, luring people, particularly children, from the surrounding churches, and kept the white dollars flowing in. The founder of one was something of a local hero and after several years of mixed results, faded from the street scene and moved on, donating the building and programs to an unconnected church across town. Variations of this happened to the other sites as well. Meantime, the under-resourced black churches soldier on. Any casual observer would conclude that the white folk's passion for poor is commendable but the strategy...not so much.

Here is the Backbreaker: If a Church as the Solution for Ministry In the Suburbs, Why Wouldn't the Black Church Be the Solution for the City? Why is that So Hard to See?

Remember the Survivalists and their limited literacy? At Dynamic Deliverance Cathedral, we don't use paper much. We are loud, verbal, musical and Biblical. The Bible is read out loud, expounded loudly, made memorable in song and illustration, and is expected to change lives. We stand in reverence when it is read. Progress in discipleship is accomplished by a series of job requirements in the church. One can begin as an Evangelist, then move to the Usher Board, to Teacher, Elder, Deacon, Minister, Reverend, Pastor and ultimately Bishop. Each step of the way, growth is expected. Disciples are made in black church, but in the Survivalist context with guidance from the Intentionalsts! Without disciple making, it would not have survived all these years. Admittedly, not all churches are thriving, but in many ways black church is done better with more influence on its people than white church.

The large point I want to make now is that **white folk GROSSLY under-estimate what black church is and what goes on there**. A bit later, I will discuss further how the *growing* black church is a key to the future. Again, I am using the term ***black church*** to denote a African-American *controlled* congregation, with a majority of attendees being people of color. There are some churches that "act white" and seem bound to deny their heritage. Thankfully they are the exception and there are few of them.

I should add that obtaining the means to leave the city and move in to the suburbs is often driven by a desire for peace and safety. While safety in the city depends on one's neighbors, safety in a gated suburb depends on distance and alarm systems. The 'burbs can insulate people from each other but at a high price. **The race to get the means to live well has more side effects than a TV drug advertisement!** So white (sometimes black) churches in the suburbs may well be substantially less about faith in God and more about stuff than their black city counterparts. Oh, I am not blind to the women who dress up in beautiful clothes at Dynamic Deliverance or the desire of the members to go to church in a fine car. But I think they have very different reasons for doing so than their suburban counterparts. Seeing those differences and understanding them is what cross-cultural efforts are about.

MYTH 3: My "Theology" Can and Will Stay the Same.

As I began to befriend young men on the street, I found that the Calvinism of my youth was a bit lacking. I had responded to the ***Total Depravity of Man*** concept as a youth and carried that image for a long time. As I evaluated myself, I believed that I started with zero value and was worthless. That is perhaps a misunderstanding of the intent of Calvin, but it made it much easier to grasp that I needed to be ***saved.***

However, that message did not play well on the streets of Baltimore. The men on the streets did not want to hear from one more source that they were simply...NOTHING! The term is Nihilism, or "nothingness." For the young man standing on the corner trying to sell drugs as part of a gang, there is nothing in polite society to affirm him. He has failed at education, is the "bad guy" in all the Hollywood movies, has experienced very limited love and frankly, has an extremely limited future. If he is not one of the 300+ who are murdered, he may be part of the 1500-2000 who are shot on the streets of Baltimore every year. Even a minimum wage job may be unobtainable if he has a prison record and a drug habit. So what is the Gospel for him?

Simply that he does have worth. Jesus died for him! So the connection to God is one of hope not shame. **That worth is evidenced by the care offered to him by God's people**. False hope, as offered by those far from the street, is not helpful. But relationships are. Not just a few minutes a week from some suburban folks who don't understand him, but the constant relationships with the church in the neighborhood...over time. The phrase from John 10:10, "The thief comes to steal, kill and destroy; but I am come that you might have Life and that more abundantly" offers hope beyond hope. It does take some convincing, but love does win!!!

Here is my conceptual point to start: **Theology and Sociology should be BFFs** (best friends forever). But, of course, they are not. In fact, to hear some people talk, sociology, a study of how people relate and group, is not worthy of consideration. But if God made people in his Image, why wouldn't we want to study them? The reason is a presupposition made by some that the Bible should be the defining document for all of humanity and should be applied without regard for culture, despite all the culture contained therein. Perhaps we need to think a bit more about that.

Cities are all about the grouping and functioning of many people. Cities are alive, moving and changing all the time. Sadly, it is a rare church, be it black or white, that moves in response to social change. One of the ironies of USA Christianity is that people are expected to change to enter a church group, but the group itself need not change because people's needs change!! Discipleship is about change, but the organizations formed by those same disciples are not expected to change. I am not speaking to specific points in this section about theological change, but I am aiming to comfort those brave enough to address irony, paradox and reality.

I want to comfort the afflicted and afflict the comfortable in the following:

I have known Pastor/Writer Brian McLaren, founder of Cedar Ridge Community Church, for many years and have been personally blessed by the ministry of him and his wife. A recent idea from him is that people tend to read the Bible in many different ways and bring a number of personal expectations to their study. However, people tend to group by how they approach the Bible and how they think it should be interpreted. He uses the term "interpretive community" and I like it a lot. Some communities are very aggressive at trying to impose their interpretation upon the world at large. Others are very passive-aggressive. Some work very hard at nailing down every question and concept; others are more "liberal." What adds to the mix is the politicization of those interpretive communities to the point where the country has resorted itself into neighborhoods that espouse a political view attached to a Biblical view or non-view (The book, *The Big Sort*, by Bill Bishop studies this in some detail). From the witchcraft trials of Massachusetts to the Scopes trial to gay rights, the various issues are very divisive when viewed from an interpretive community perspective. None of this is helpful for the student of the city. That is not to say that the city is unfriendly to different opinion. There is always room for differences. But those differences don't particularly translate into relationships across cultural and organized religion lines.

From my experience, the softening of hard politics and strict doctrine is necessary to influence the larger city. A thoughtful person might observe that the current "red" States, are mostly rural and the "blue" States are mostly urban. I found that as a Republican from a "red" state living in a very staunch "blue" State, it was in my personal interest as well as the Gospel's that I reconsider some of my beliefs. **Actually, it is about my understanding of how others see things and what drives their values that I am looking for.**

One of the side effects of a humble, learner who makes a serious attempt at BEING in the city is the **eventual failure of some part of their theological framework**. That is a difficult pill indeed. For many people, it is the observed neediness as demonstrated by the crime statistics, sad stories, debauchery, drugs, murders and the like, that causes the well-intentioned to consider working for Jesus in the city. As one gets involved in the lives of the people, it often becomes apparent that the atonement-centered Gospel has been there before them.

When I began doing property rehabs, I discovered that all my guys had "prayed to receive Christ." I somewhat sarcastically call it the "Magic Words" approach. Some believe the saying/praying of certain words will make one a Christian, including being baptized. But, I discovered that such actions had little effect on their crack or heroin addiction. They did mean it at the time and wanted life to change, but It did little for their job status, love life or their community.

In fact, I believe it is one of the great myths of our time that the city is much more un-Godly than the surrounding suburbs. As I look outward from the city, I fear more for the suburbs than the city. When I make these assertions, I find few white folks in agreement. It simply doesn't fit their paradigm. We have always been taught in Evangelical and Fundamentalist circles that the city is bad and the farm is good. Not so, in my experience. There is evil afoot in many a farm community these days. Unlike whites, non-practicing black people are not hostile about God. Church is at the very heart and tradition of black culture. I found, "Through the Storm, Through the Night" by Paul Harvey (not the white radio guy), a Professor at the University of Colorado at Colorado Springs to be a concise and helpful short volume on the subject. So what does your theology have to say about addiction? Particularly what does it say to people who are not in control of their lives?

Here is an example of a theological point: Many feel that Paul's "If any man be in Christ, he is a new Creation" is **prescriptive**. I was taught so in my youth. The evidence of a real Christian is a changed life. As it turns out, it isn't always. I am part of a church, Dynamic Deliverance Cathedral, which believes that God CAN heal. And He can. And He does frequently there. I have seen it with my own eyes in a service or two. But not everyone and not all. We recently buried a man who had been healed of AIDS and was a clean addict. But after some years of health and clean urine, he "went back out" and started up with drugs again. When his health failed from crack abuse, his AIDS come back with a vengeance. Despite all the tears and multiple repentance, he finally died as multiple organs failed. Per the prescription, he should not have "gone back out." But he did.

When I think about it, it makes sense to me to see Paul's statement as generally **Descriptive** rather than **PREscriptive**. It is not easy for us to determine who is a Christian and who is not. Of course, we get hints from changes in a person's life, but not always. Some change is hard in coming. And most of us have some sin that refuses to die properly. Further, change is not forever. "A man convinced against his will, is of the same opinion still" as the adage goes. Sometimes convictions don't last. I wonder if the problem is that we don't always see the big picture when we read the Bible, particularly as a young believer. I cringe when I hear word for word expositions of Bible documents, particularly the Old Testament. When I hear someone remark, "JESUS CHRIST!" I must look for the context, it can be either a prayer or a curse!

My friend Brian McLaren has dared to suggest that the Bible may be less of a "Constitutional" document and more of a "public library." That has not won him friends in all circles. I think the human tendency is to continuously work to refine God and his purpose into ever *smaller* circles as we get older. We seem to take delight in determining what is IN and what is OUT of those circles. I don't wish to elaborate a whole lot on this general topic. I am not interested in arguments with professional Bible-arguers.

Instead, I want to affirm those folks who venture into the city or cross-cultural ministry **and** experience some failure of their former theological presuppositions. What would you do if the Spirit grabbed you in one of several ways? What if you suddenly found yourself on your knees speaking in tongues? How would you explain it? If one comes from an interpretive community that requires signed doctrinal statements, including a self-confessing clause that if the person changes ANY of those beliefs in the slightest, they must report such to a ruling body for adjudication and possible expulsion, it is tough.

How do you change to meet the situation if your paycheck depends on your NOT changing?

Over the years, I have gotten a number of 'missions' types aside and got them "talking turkey." Many admit they have seen and heard things that have changed them greatly, but they cannot share with their donors. The God they have experienced doesn't fit into the box their donors have created with all the theological trappings. This may happen to YOU, as you engage the city.

Changes of strategy?

While I am in the general vicinity, let me observe a couple things about how ministry is often begun. Typically the flow is:

GET A MESSAGE *(possibly a combination of Good News and a political statement)*

GET A METHOD *(like church-planting)*

FIND A COMMUNITY TO WORK IN

Ever think about how it would work if we switched the order? Suppose we started by:

BUILDING RELATIONSHIPS IN A COMMUNITY WE RESONATE WITH

CONSIDER WAYS TO BE HEARD AND DISCIPLE

WORK UP AND CONTINUOUSLY REVISE THE MESSAGE — WE CHOOSE TO BE IN THAT COMMUNITY *(Telling is overrated)*

Might presence be more effective? More about "being Jesus" later.

Indeed, this switch is the heart of the **Neighboring Movement,** that is gaining momentum.

Let's look at the thinking process again:

For some who understand by comparing, consider the following about convictions, assertions and absolutes:

1. CONSIDERATION IS NOT CONVICTION—I grew up in a Christian world that ascribed evil intent to people *thinking* about a counter-theology to certain convictions they held. It made sense until I got older and ended up simply dropping a number of convictions…without replacing them. In my younger days, I was anxious to have "convictions" on nearly everything from footwear to Bible translation. That was a bit cumbersome of a couple levels. Someone coined the phrase, "flexible theology" which was meant as an insult but made sense to me. I decided to only have a "conviction" if forced into it. And then it had to work 100%, all the time. For example, I thought the idea of women in leadership, church or parachurch, was a bad idea, even un-Biblical. Then I had a couple female supervisors who changed my mind. Karen was not only a great Bible teacher but a great boss. I could trust her with my thoughts and know she would make a good decision. She may have been the best supervisor I ever had. You may know her as the Urbana Missions Convention Operations Director for about 20 years in the 1980's and 1990's. And there were others that I wished I could work for. Had they been my leadership, I might have lasted longer in full-time ministry. So, I dropped my objection to women in

leadership. Who wouldn't like to work for someone who understood them, was spiritually centered, very wise, not manipulative, extremely knowledgeable, creative, organized and quietly enthusiastic? Did I replace my original, "Biblical conviction"? No, I just placed it in **the consideration** pile, not **the conviction** pile. I have since met several women pastors who should *not* have been assigned a church, but that is another issue. **I am just not convinced that gender alone is sufficient to deny a leadership role for *anyone*, nor is it a good reason to promote.**

2. **INVESTIGATION IS NOT CONCLUSION**—Recently there has been some work done on the concepts of Heaven and Hell. Some, like Rob Bell, former Pastor of the Mars Hill Bible Church in Michigan who wrote a book called, "Love Wins," have placed their *investigative* thoughts on paper with the obvious implications. A chunk of Christianity assumed his thoughts were *conclusions* and reacted inappropriately. He was forced to resign from his pastor role for the good of his people. He simply was not prepared of the wild assumptions that people made from his investigations and thoughts. A fourth of his church left after the book was published. Of course, such investigations challenge people who have a theology that is strongly and narrowly atonement-theory based. What is missed, of course, is that careful re-considerations and investigations can lead to greater appreciation of the Gospel, not lesser. I think the serious city people worker will always be investigating things that don't seem to fit. This book is written as though it is conclusionary, but I cannot be sure that my data is exhaustive…because I keep finding more to consider that can radically change my views. Why? Because I simply don't know the depth of the Body of Knowledge that God offers through His Spirit. I don't know how much I don't know.

3. **PROPOSITIONS ARE NOT NECESSARILY ABSOLUTE TRUTH**—As Westerners, we are well schooled in the concept of propositional truth. We apply that to the Bible, as though it were a tech manual to be "de-coded." Many people use a concordance, which looks for the same word across the 66 documents that make up today's Protestant Bible. Never mind the changes in Bible culture, style, communication tools, and author's intent. No one seems to mind that the Bible has effectively been re-written into a "systematic theology" which extracts certain concepts from verses that may not have been part of the author's real purpose. Instead, those re-writes turn into theological propositions, like Calvin's "Institutes," vast arrays of commentaries, and defended opinions. Heavy weight is given to the "literal" meaning of phrases, parables and opinions of Bible writers. Sometimes even Jesus' clearest teaching, like John 13:34, 35 gets overlooked as the arguments over the propositional fine point turn personal and insulting.

Here has been my key experience. For at least the last 20 years, I have heard very few sermons I could completely agree with. In contrast to the consumer-based training most people receive, i.e. "shop" for a "good" church and leave if they don't like something that was said or done, I get to be slightly irritated every Sunday! I deal with it by focusing on what I can glean from a service as I worship with others who love God. I dwell on what we share, not what we don't share. I also work at not forming opinions on everything. To the person who says, "Christians must take a position and have a conviction," I say, "No, thank you." I focus on my ever-growing relationship with Jesus, everything else is up for discussion. I tend to look for the Spirit of God, not the work of Satan. As a church real estate agent, I attend the meetings of the disbanding churches as well as the meetings of the growing churches. I find God in both groups. In fact, He is at work all over Baltimore!!! If the names of Rob Bell or Brian Mclaren cause you to flip-your-cookies, *and* you claim a call to the city, you may be in for some crumbling…though certainly not from either of them!

4. **WE DON'T MAKE ADEQUATE ROOM FOR PARADOX**—How do you explain two totally opposite concepts that should be exclusive but are not? If we are honest, by our rationale, much of the Bible is in tension. How can Jesus be both God and Man? Not possible, it is like being little bit pregnant. How can God be both loving and judgmental? How can my sins be forgiven but I still have a tendency to sin? So we have a Hellenistic view which requires us to explain the paradoxes and to explain the Trinity by dissection of function! How can God and Jesus be both in our hearts and in Heaven at the same time? I vote for the notion of a "**spiderweb**" as a visualization of doctrine instead of the popular "**wall**" concept. Spiderwebs are anchored at many opposite points, yet there is a relationship between them all. Because they are anchored but also in tension, the webs are very strong. We tend to move between the points as we live life, if on anchor seems to fail, it is of no consequence, there more. Does your theology really have to be linear and symmetrical?

5. **CONTEXT CONTROLS MEANING, NOT THE DICTIONARY**—This is a big one for the literalist. I'm sure you have heard the term, ***The Word of God***. I can think of at least 6 meanings of the term.

- John 1 the ***Word of God*** is Jesus
- The ***Word*** came to a variety of people in the Old Testament, as a still small voice, etc.
- The term in some places of the New Testament refers to the Old Testament.
- Some folks in the New Testament were given a prophetic "Word."

- And, of course, the Pastor gets up on Sunday and says "I believe I have a *Word* from the Lord today."
- And then there is a claim that the 66 documents put together by the Catholic Church in various forms over the years, AKA the "Bible," is "the Word of God."

So the term, "Word or Word of God" has a wide usage, some of them a bit more accurate than others. So what is the context usage?

Again, one of the burdens to bear when doing ministry WITH churches is that you will encounter people whose theology is shaky...including your own!

Chapter 6

Secret Windows to look through

Enough of the negatives. Ready for some windows to discover and perhaps open wide?

SECRET WINDOW 1: Asset-Based, Holistic Ministry Rather than Only Needs Based.

Translating that into a city effort, suppose we began by attending churches in a area. Suppose we asked the people what they thought the ASSETS of the community were? Based on those assets, suppose we moved to capitalize on them in some way? As we made those strengthening moves WITH the community, suppose we moved people toward discipleship in a way that made sense to them? Remember, the largest asset of a community is its PEOPLE!

About 20 years ago, I met Navigator Jeff Dennis and the folks working in West side of Chicago. They had chosen to live among city people and to respond to the needs around them by building relationships and thinking big. The men and women there needed jobs and stability for their families, but there were problems with finding and keeping them. Jeff and his friends saw the people as assets to their community, not liabilities. They figured out that by building up a "job factory" they could offer a message in the context of capitalizing on those assets. So at "Breaking Ground," they offer jobs, job training and housing development.

To me, "giveaways" seem to make more sense when used to complement an asset instead of highlighting failure. In short, I approve of a "marriage" between the Giveaways and the Interactives, but recommend a church wedding! (Giveaways and Interactives BELONG in Church!!) I observe that our society has managed to teach the poor to present the worst sides of themselves to get the "goodies." Ever noticed that the panhandler holding the cardboard sign goes to great lengths to look pathetic? A recent favorite was the person holding a sign that said "Hungry, Homeless, Can You Help"... while eating a sandwich!

Jeff and his folks looked for people who had potential to work but lacked the training and certification do get a job. Think about it. Most programs only help needy people directly, not the able-bodied, ready-to-work. Really? How did that become the standard? How has that been working out?

One of the techniques of the Community Organizer movement is to ask communities and the people in them what they are GOOD at. People respond very differently to people interested in highlighting their abilities than they do to "get" whatever is being given away. I find that when I complement people in the city for what they do well or for what I like about WHO they are, I get big smiles. Contrast that with all the sad faces on the fund-raising folks who make up the cardboard signs, stand on the street corner, and post themselves for solicitation!

But to discover the assets of a community you will have to do so WITH them. You will need involvement, research and relationships.

SECRET WINDOW 2: Get on the Holy Ghost Train!

As we have the Sunday Service at Dynamic Deliverance Cathedral, Bishop frequently guides the order of worship by announcing, **"We are gonna move this Holy Ghost Train on to the next Stop!"** We all know what that means. At this point we are feeling the Presence of Jesus via the Holy Ghost and look forward to the next blessing that will surely show up.

If we weave the notion that some theological changes are likely when one tries to be authentic in city ministry, perhaps we need to highlight an addition…the **work of the Spirit**. A part of the white culture is the defining people not so much as WHO they are but what they DO. I find most successful white people will tell me what they DO, WHO they know, and what they have ACCOMPLISHED. Their evidence is heavily weighted toward introducing me to their accumulated STUFF, trophies, etc. Getting some idea of WHO they are is a bit more difficult. As I get older, I notice my contemporaries tend to define themselves by their various medical deficiencies! But in general, people in the USA don't deal much with who they are, although some will define who they are by their religious or political beliefs.

One of the things I have learned from the kind folks at Dynamic Deliverance is that **WHO I am is transmitted by my spirit.** To them, my presence is felt for WHO I am, much more than what I DO. For the last 10 years or so, the most I DO in the church is to attend some meetings, preach once a year on a Friday night and sometimes I get to pray for the offering!! It is my friendship with Bishop Adams, his extended family and friendships with all the people I have gotten to know in the church that seem to be what is most appreciated. Over and over people come up to me and say, "we feel when you are here" and "miss you when you are gone." It makes sense in a church of survivalists, but not for the Intentionalist. It has puzzled me for years, because I have been well trained to be judged on what I do, not who I am. In my Calvinist heart, I struggle to believe that somehow I am really Spirit-filled and that others can feel it. Yet I am continuously presented with anecdotal evidence that WHO I am precedes me on the streets of Baltimore.

As I mention early in the next "window," I did a lot of my initial city connections in a wounded condition. I felt I had little to offer. Ralph said, while doing some reflecting the other day, "We saw that you were a landlord but we knew God sent you." How? In my mind, I needed to have a program, be a shining leader, or perform miracles. I guess the miracle was that I stuck with it. But God somehow came through. We all need to understand how the Spirit works in connecting people. And then use our faith.

Suppose for the moment that anyone on the street can read the Spirit in me. I know intellectually that I am the Temple for the person of Jesus via the Spirit. Suppose it is that Spirit that is helpful, more helpful than all the stuff I do. So what is the real message? "Do what I tell you to" or "be like me and ……?" Not easy answers when you must live life among people BEING who you are. Much easier to just preach something or tell others what to do. We use the term, "incarnation," but don't really grasp the importance of it in our intellectually based (or so we think) white society. But our real love is in our hug, in how our face lights up when we greet someone, and in how we transmit our expectations.

Now if you are like I was, this whole "Holy Ghost" thing was NOT what I wanted to mess with. I was a feet-on-the- floor Baptist as well as a Presbyterian Elder…doing things decently and in order. I hated having some fool try to mess with my emotions, implying I should have more of them… But as I understood the people at Dynamic Deliverance, I understood the "why" for their exuberance. I felt it and appreciated that I was a part of that as well. On any Sunday morning, you will see people up and jumping…and people just sitting in the pew. All are accepted and welcome to worship in their way. Even I am free to 'loosen up' and do a bit of 'shouting'. (That is an insider term, yours to discover).

A "Holy Ghost Party" may well be totally foreign to you. Think of it this way. Suppose each Sunday, you brought your part of "God in you" and put it in the mix of Church that day. Suppose worship, praise and learning that day became the sum of all those Spirit contributions and MORE! Suppose ALL your needs were met as you contributed, confessed, celebrated, learned and committed yourself. All in a safe place. Suppose this thing became all about an encouraged heart AND an encouraged head. Sound good? Happens every Sunday at Dynamic Deliverance Cathedral, 630 North Linwood, Baltimore, MD.

I want to highlight, then, two parts to this Holy Ghost experience.

FIRST, **my sense of Spirit in other people has been greatly sharpened.** I began to see that Spirit-led people can often **sense what they cannot see**. I can see reflections in another's face what their heart is processing. I can FEEL the absence of a healthy spirit and their desire to move closer to God. It happens in an instant, much quicker than an observation-analysis can occur. Yet, I feel like a rookie in this experience. I have seen what a prophetic gift is like and I don't have that.

SECOND, **I have a greater sense of *collective* spirit.** I, too, can *feel* the collected contributions of Spirit that each person brings to worship. Each Friday night and each Sunday, we gather together in different combinations with different experiences to worship. It is never the same from one time to another. If heaven is like that…I can take the Forever Life!

SECRET WINDOW 3: The Death of GREAT EXPECTATIONS

Remember my questions earlier about your expectations?

I recommend you do your best to **KILL THEM!**

When I talk to folks who want to *do something in the city* I frequently tell them, "First, go ahead and kill every one of your expectations!" That seldom thrills them. People are driven by all sorts of plans, dreams and schemes. All are of the highest and pure motives, at least to that person. Yet, I can remember the day the very last of my dreams died. Even where I was standing when it died and I realized it was my last one. My van was stolen in broad daylight on a Saturday in the heart of Baltimore City. It held desperately needed supplies for a job that I desperately needed to get done Monday because I desperately needed the money. My real estate and landlording efforts had passed from life support to being unplugged. My white church, if they were honest, hated me. I was yet to be embraced by black church. I had teenagers facing college and no funds to pay for it. In the world of aviation we say, "When you run out of airspeed, altitude and ideas all at the same time, you are in trouble!!" That was me. Even my wife had some reservations about me and how things were going. And there I was standing on the street in the inner city of Baltimore with no ideas, no dreams and not a whole lot of hope and no work van. That event signified to me that I was out of expectations. Only God could somehow give direction to life.

It was so pathetic it was amusing! I was laughing, somewhat insanely, that ONLY God could help me now! And slowly, beginning with discovery of my stolen van late that night, which had all the copper pipe and an air conditioning condensing unit still in it, things began to improve. It was all those losses that freed my spirit to empathize a little bit with the people I knew in the city. It was that sense of helplessness and fatalism that helped me feel how useless my expectations really were. For an Intentionalist person to begin understanding what the Survivalist must deal with daily, they often need to lose all those intentions and gain faith. How else will an Intentionalist understand, unless they experience, however temporarily, the need to just survive?

I often marvel at how much "Biblical" justification it seems to take for the "haves" to interact with the "have-nots" in a Christian setting! It should take very little. I see people spend $50,000 on a new SUV without batting an eye, but ask them to help at a Black Church or city event and they need to do an extensive "Bible Study" to get the "Biblical View of Justice." **Shouldn't they do a Bible Study on "Spending Money vs Investing in People" instead?**

There is ample data of the differences between the minority/majority urban world. Remember the term *hypersegregation*? In 1954, after the Brown Vs. Board of Education, Supreme Court Decision, the Baltimore City schools moved toward desegregation. The school system student population at the time was 60% white and 40% black, with the black students concentrated in a few areas. Recently, enrollment data showed the Baltimore schools were 8% white, with the white students concentrated in a few schools. In short, by any stretch of the imagination, the schools are still segregated, even more than they were in 1954.

What progress has really been made?

Two Other Areas Remain Segregated.

Undertaking and Church!! Whites don't use black funeral directors for some strange reason. Whites don't go to black church, for reasons they don't explain to themselves.

I suspect the cause is:

- UNCOMFORTABLE FORMS OF WORSHIP

- NOT IDENTIFYING WITH THE PEOPLE

- THE PRESENCE OF SURVIVALISTS

- SUPREME RELUCTANCE TO INTEGRATE BASED ON RACE ALONE

- THE DISCOMFORT OF NOISY WORSHIP! *(...perhaps)*

- GUILT

There I said it. **I believe guilt to be a worthless emotion when it comes to race, since it seems to act as a barrier to conciliation** *(Reconciliation* *implies there was a relationship to start with. So actually, there is no such thing as **Racial Reconciliation!**). I believe guilt has no place in the Church and certainly is no basis for Segregation.*

But there is a secret outsiders don't know about black church. It is about soothing your soul. If you can just drag your beat-up self into black church on Sunday for a strong dose of Praise, you will be OK for at least a few days!! Or at least in some churches. They deal with chronic people all the time and know that a dose of the Holy Ghost may not cure all your ills, but will at least make you forget them for a while and let you focus on Jesus!

SECRET WINDOW 4: Unmasking the ACTION GAP

If you don't have a good working definition of what ministry really is, you may have trouble deciding what to do. Part of the reason for this book is to help the reader gain understanding of the city and the other is to help focus their connection to it. And hopefully offer a couple ways to look at plausible ministry.

My observation is that white folks desperately hope that their **intentions** will translate into acceptable **actions**. During times of relative "prosperity" in an organization, which is a time where the Ministry Train seems confined to the tracks and moving at an acceptable rate of speed, it is common for organizations to look around and see the need for minority ministry. Various inputs, often provoking guilt, convince senior leadership that some major efforts need to put into minority ministry, which can include "under-resourced" people. No problem with that. Better late than never.

But let something happen to the train already on the tracks and the attention (read people, funds and initiative) will be shifted back to **that** train, not the construction of new tracks or the sharing of their existing tracks with a minority rail company. If a funding source dries up, a capital investment needs to be made, a character flaw is discovered, some shift in government policy, or anything perceived as threatening the train schedule, those issues will get taken care of first. Because the real goals of an organization in the USA include **the preservation of the Corporation** as the Number 1 task of the leadership, everything else must take a back seat. We know that if something (or someone) threatens our donor stream, it has got to go! No one talks about it, but significant decisions are made to accept or reject certain ministry efforts because of potential donor disapproval. I can't name the names or issues in this paper, it might deflect my point, but they are there. Conservative Christians, as the title implies, are not particularly forgiving when it comes to certain issues.

So, any sacrifice made on the part of the majority for the sake of the minorities is important. Promises kept under difficult circumstances prove that the organization is serious, not just hopeful. I found that if I said I would do something, it was very important to the survivalist that I do so…because NOT keeping promises is more of the norm for majority Intentionalists.

In their minds, INTENTION is almost as good as the real thing when it pertains to engaging survivalists. Perhaps you think I am being a bit harsh. I have had many years of watching people proclaim their desire to "engage the city" only to have disappeared in a couple years. I watch churches "reach out to the homeless," which means they take sandwiches, chips and soda pop to the homeless area of the city and hand it out. They report with great excitement that souls were saved, the hungry were fed and Satan beaten back. The following week they do it again. But in a precious few months, they stop coming and are nowhere to be found. **It turns out that the homeless are a rather tough lot**. They are perfectly willing to take anything given to them and willing to talk with people…if the goodies hold out. But the people who drive in from the suburban churches are not prepared to understand the world of the homeless, much less to be conversant in it. What do you discuss with a person sleeping on a bench? You must get into their world, not expect them to come to yours. Not easily done. So as reality sets in, the outsider church folk step back out. Meantime, the homeless go to the churches in the area, as they have always done…if they want to do church. And the Rescue Mission is only 2 blocks away, where they can get the message AND food AND a bed if they attend.

TWO Quick Tips About the Homeless.

1. Want To Know If the Person Holding a Sign Up Begging for Food or Money is Really Homeless?

Get out of your car and smell them! The truly homeless who live outside have a very distinct smell. In short, they stink! If they don't stink, chances are they have some place to stay that has showers! They may wear clothes that say otherwise, but the smell won't lie!

2. Want to Really Help Them…But Don't Know if They are Legit?

Don't respond at the time but set an appointment to talk with them later or the next day. If they show up at the appointed time, they are serious about accepting help to change. I think that what we want to do is help those who are desperately looking for it. Some are desperate to get out of their mess. No way will they miss an appointment with someone who really cares. Because the person who will give them a couple bucks and walk away…often doesn't really care about them, they just feel sorry or guilty. In my opinion, just giving money to people simply re-enforces unhelpful behavior. To get your money, they must focus on their needs, not their assets.

How is that helpful?

SECRET WINDOW 5: Identify Your Self-Interest

Unless you know your **why** you will **fade when stretched by your city efforts**. This is a variation of the question of expectations. With a little different angle.

There is an adage that simply says, **"People do what they want to do."** Intentionalists set their own goals and agendas, so for them to choose to work at ethnic connections, they will have to see a more compelling reason to do so than what they are currently doing. Monocultural people need motivation to pay the price of becoming cross-cultural, even on a small level. So we need to think of what the advantages are.

If we think about it, we are all created in the "Image of God," yet each of us does not encompass the whole of God. For many of us, to know God is our earthly goal. It follows that if we are serious about that, we need to find those parts of God that are in other people but not in us! In short, the over-riding reason for crossing any kind of cultural divide is simply to know God! That should be compelling enough, but there is a bit more to it.

It was suggested that there are five motivations for Intentionalists:

1. **REWARDS.** Look again at the Isaiah 58: "then shall your light rise in the darkness and your gloom be as the noonday. And the lord will guide you continually and satisfy your desire in scorched places and make your bones strong; and you shall be like a watered garden, like a spring of water whose waters do not fail. And your ancient ruins shall be rebuilt; and you shall raise up the foundations of many generations; you shall be called the repairer of the breach, the restorer of streets to dwell in." Wow, what a DEAL!! I find that very motivating!!! Of course I need to DO and BE the verses that precede the rewards.

2. **PUNISHMENT.** NOT getting a reward is a punishment, but the most major to me is the separation from the work of God. I have had the pleasure of enjoying the hand of God, seeing his fingerprints in the lives of people and seeing miracles. To NOT enjoy that is a torture most feared. I sometime use the "analogy of proximity."

If you really loved Barack Obama, would you move closer to the White House or further away? I can imagine a hater moving to Alaska, north of the Arctic Circle and living in a cave with no radio, TV, or Internet. If you loved Obama, then moving to that cave would be a punishment most cruel and severe. Conversely, the true lover of Obama could not get close enough. I see the same in the pursuit of God. It is a form of punishment for me to simply stand pat. I hope it is for you also.

3. **ALTRUISM.** I think total altruism is a rather elusive for most of us. Even when I want to do something without expecting something in return, I remember II Cor. 15:58, my defining life verse from the WhingDing of 1965, "your labor is not in vain in the Lord" What does seem to be rewarding is to know that God will be Glorified if I am obedient. The more I believe this and act upon it, the more rewarding that feeling becomes. And the more I understand who God is. Of course, that is not exactly altruism, but it feels like it.

4. **JUST PLAIN BLESSING.** What does the "blessing of God" look like? About 15 years ago, as I discovered Bishop Adams and Dynamic Deliverance Cathedral, things were more difficult. Friendships, national ministry connections, finances, family and work were all in a bit of a turmoil. As I begin to give time, money and energy to the ministry of that church, all that changed. ALL OF IT! It is a bit like having frosting coat all your life! God became more real, marriage became more unified, my understanding of city ministry started coming together, money began to flow, enjoyable situations became the norm, old dreams became reality, and my children began to prosper. I am overwhelmed by the goodness of God! By any count, I stand to gain as I move closer to the work of God in black church. And that has been my experience. My costs have been more than repaid by the spiritual rewards and presence of God himself. If your investment pays off BIG, over time, you are no fool to have invested.

5. **THE GOD YOU DON'T KNOW—YET!** If your view of God is large enough to embrace all the people of the world then you will understand just how much of God you don't know! So, this may be about your passion to know God as much as possible and not just serve Him. I am a Servant of the Most High. But my eyes are not on just my efforts to serve, but on the Master. In fact, we both look through my eyes in both a physical and spiritual sense and SEE! That is available to you as well, but you will have to interact with people who are different from you to see it.

SECRET WINDOW 6: It's All About the CHURCH.

Mega-churches have cost us neighborhoods. Like WalMart, their attractions eliminate the competition. We don't produce pastors of a limited parish, we produce pastors who want a career path that ends at the top of the given interpretive community. Whether white church or black church, the young want growth and change, the old want stability and consistency. Neighborhoods are messy, filled with goofy people. A nice, clean church filled with high achievers, high quality worship and a large parking lot is a likely result of imitating the liturgy of the USA shopping mall. The next time you go to a modern shopping mall, notice how much it is like a Mega-church, or vice versa. First, huge parking lot. That's because no one walks, everyone needs a car or bus to get there. There is an appealing entrance, with a directory and help-desk just inside. You are asked what you are looking for. A sumptuous buffet of classes, meetings, kid interests, and the coming attractions await. Neat, clean, plenty of restrooms, changing rooms, excellent music, friendly people, etc. Clean, thoughtful, credit-worthy *shoppers* will feel at home in either place.

How can a small scruffy neighborhood church compete? In the same way the neighborhood store has given way to the mega-store and even the Internet, the church on the nearest corner is begging for help like a hallway full of the wheelchair bound folks at a nursing home!

Yet, we will all end up in a church…somewhere. We all live in a neighborhood. We hope that we can somehow fit in and be recognized. We need to get the family "marrying and burying" duties done …somewhere. The survivalist with no friends, no transportation, no money and no hope is depending on any interpretive community that will have him…if he can find one. In my opinion, the para-church, task specific group, cannot take the place of the church in city neighborhoods. Now I am *not* trying to criticize your favorite group. I am suggesting there are structural limitations for any and all that are outside a local church . Their focus is too narrow, their people are not broad enough, and they have little real investment there. People who do work in an ethnic specific community should expect to attend and be a part of a church in that community. Putting another way, I think a *huge* call is necessary to **justify ministry apart from a local church**. If you are moving in that direction, I suggest it be a *growing* church. Non-growing churches have another set of problems that are not helpful to a community. Generally they are prepared to give out but are needy themselves.

But do understand that some churches are small, but they are *producing* churches. The existing system of how black churches grow encourages people to grow and as their gifts develop, to start a storefront church themselves. Some churches remain small but help their gifted to start up a church. They can be very helpful to be a part of.

Respect For Black Church Is Mandatory

Think about this—remember that the highest value of the USA African-American subculture is *dignity & respect*? **If we don't respect the black church, what are we saying**? If we are ignorant of the tremendous effect of black church on black culture, don't we look like fools? If we refuse to be a part of that, isn't that an insult? I suspect the average white person cannot name a black pastor of national prominence, after they get past Pastor Tony Evans. (I am taking nothing away from Pastor Evans, I just tire of his being the only one people know) So when white folk began to appreciate black church, it has a lot of impact. Granted, the cable TV may not be much help. When in Iowa recently, I was asking about some BET programs. Turns out that since Iowa is still 91% white, ethnic programing is not a priority!

I notice that white organizations often don't know the black church leaders in cities so they assume they are free to do whatever they want. Which, of course, they are, but not following protocols can retard relationships. Can you learn to be part of more than one kind of church and more than one kind of *interpretive community? Of course*! But it will require some change of thinking and some new experiences.

As a side note here, I often wish I could video what I see at Dynamic Deliverance. But I don't. I just don't think it is for outsiders to understand. It is a little like seeing intimacy that shouldn't be seen by others. I see the response of people to God as though no one else can see. It is very humbling and not for spiritual voyeurs. But that is also the conflict, that if you don't learn to understand, you will miss the blessing!

When Narrow Thinking Hurts...

My observation is that the white church at large deals with the problems and possibilities that are beyond its influence by creating parachurch, 501 (C) (3), groups and often ignores the indigenous church. Or, it invites people of color to join them in white church on their terms. But in their hearts they believe **their** interpretive community to be superior to the city minority church. Paternalism, anyone, ...anyone?

I believe that the **key to the urban church in the future is white folks that will join them, bringing their money and their presence.** At this point I probably know over 30 black churches and pastors through my efforts in real estate sales. None of them object to an influx of white folks. It is the simplest, most meaningful gift that can be given, a **ministry of presence**. A white person with a smile and a desire to affirm is worth their weight in Kingdom gold. A white person with urban preparation, growing cultural immersion, is even more desirable than fine gold. No joke.

It is OK to visit black churches, find one that your spirit resonates with and ask the Pastor if he minds your coming once a month or so. In fact, it is more than OK. It is what black church is about, the collective of people who praise, worship and hear the Word. It does help greatly to have a humble attitude.

Many Sundays, as I walk in the door of Dynamic Deliverance Cathedral, I am greeted by the Ushers. I am formally escorted to the platform by them and I walk down the side isle shaking hands and exchanging greetings. On the platform, I greet the other pastors who hug me gladly or extend their hand. Bishop Adams gives me a hug and I take my place on his right or left. I wave at the various band members who are usually playing but acknowledge me with a smile and a nod. I look over the crowd and wave or smile at various ones. The feeling comes over me that I am a very privileged person in the Kingdom of God. I get to worship with HIS people and see HIS hand in many of their lives as they come forward later in the service for prayer and healing. The presence of the Holy Ghost is palpable and leaves me in awe. I am one blessed man. I feel so sorry for those who could not join me in this revelry. It has only been going on for 14 years or so, but I am hoping for an Eternity!!

But I got there the hard way. No reason others should make the same mistakes I did. There must be a way to teach/train others.

In part I am hoping this book will be a text for that effort.

SECRET WINDOW 7: City Training in the Form of *Flight Instruction* is a Must.

We all know people who went on a *missions trip,* who crashed and burned on re-entry. Some may have even served part of an assignment before returning. It may have simply been a person walking away from the "mission field," never to look back. That is a loss for all of us. Often it is about "Culture Shock." Sooner or later, that hits.

I remember the early days of working in Baltimore City as a landlord and property rehabber. More days than I care to admit, I headed home at the end of the day with a near-hatred for the inner city. I was slammed in the face by a culture that made no sense. My entire life and existence seemed to be in the hands of "gypsies, tramps and thieves." I hated the patterns of multigenerational poverty, illegal drug sales and usage, as well as the fatalism that seemed to reduce people to beggars, manipulators and inhuman activities. It all seemed like a slow-motion train wreck and I was along for the ride!

As I began my journey there was no clear way for me to prepare for the street culture I would later embrace. Or at least I didn't know about it. Like others, I could see the negatives, but had no good perspective on the positives. I have both attended ethnic training and been an ethnicity trainer over the years. I think there are some key ingredients to understanding/overcoming one's ethnicity to embrace another.

There is no substitute for guided experience. In aviation, you cannot learn to fly a plane by workshop, lecture or reading books. You MUST be placed in the hands of a flight instructor and suitable aircraft or you will DIE!! Granted, crossing cultures is not quite as deadly, but unless both study and experience is combined, little will be learned.

White privilege must be wrestled with along with institutional racism and paternalism.

Having said that, **not everyone will learn to fly,** some just want to board the plane. We need to know their real interests and intentions. And help them to identify them. Few people really want to leave the supermarket for a neighborhood store.

People have to *want to*. I have known people who lived in the city, were warm and friendly, but were nearly oblivious to how their street worked relationally. They stayed a few years and left…leaving no neighbors in the lurch. It was as though they never lived there. They were very bright, even brilliant people, when it came to intellect, but rather dense when it came to community. And embracing the poor.

People need to be told the steps to crossing cultures. Revisit my " 7 stages" in Chapter 2. Those steps take time. One cannot simply be "assigned" to a city and told to do work, whether black, white or other. Each step means a greater commitment and a greater price. Caste or class structures in our society are very powerful and "going down" in class is very hard on one's faith, among other things. I am trying to give some of those steps in this book.

I think the **combination of individualized study, specialized individual experience and close coaching CAN shorten the learning curve for many whites**. All of us white folks who eat and breath this stuff must continue to read, attend different kinds of training and ask understanding questions of minorities who can stand us! Though this book may seem excessively long to you, trust me, there is much more to learn.

Some immersion training is recommended. The extreme may be what my buddy Ralph suggested: "Homeless training" where the trainees are given $100 and be told to survive on the streets of Baltimore for a week...with coaching, of course, but no food or housing provided! As I talked with another "street guy" he also got excited about such a program! That may be a huge jolt for some people, but for others it could be a real jump-start. Realistically, there are other ways to do immersion, the simple, gentler way is for people to stay in black church family homes in the city for a couple weeks. That is quite easy to do, benefits the black folks and has some degree of safety.

And people should be told the whole experience of city ministry might be gut-wrenching. I have many scenes vividly locked in my memory. The sight of a two-year-old child sitting vacantly on a bed with no food having been sleeping with a crack-addicted mother. Watching a black man get shot in the back by a white man as he ran from his knife assault on two Native American women. Seeing a man dead from a drive-by (actually a walk-by) shooting. Cleaning up the gooey mess from more than one tenant who died. Walking out the office door into pools of blood from a knife fight. And making the transitional understanding of an Intentionalist in relationships with many survivalists. Much anger, lots of tears, not much understanding on the part of other white folk. It can be like combat in a war. You tell ghastly stories as a way of trying to understand them yourself...when they are like a horror movie others have not seen. Be sure you can handle it. Like the following true story.

A MOTHERS SCREAM

It began with a curious phone call from a resident of one of my rental apartment buildings. "Hey, it really stinks in here" began the conversation. Since it was a Saturday night, I was not inclined to get personally involved. "We think the guy in #1 is dead!" Now I definitely was not going to run down there and get involved! Nothing I could do for him if he was dead and I didn't want to spend the next 2 or 3 hours milling around.

"Call the Police, " the resident was instructed. There were a couple more calls before the Police finally broke into the apartment and discovered that, indeed, a 25-year-old man was dead. The television was still on while he still stared at it. The Medical Examiner came for the body and I heard later that it was blamed on a "heart attack."

The next day, my buddy and I stopped by. The doors and windows were open, though all the former resident's possessions were untouched... defended by the smell. We grabbed the TV, VCR, video games and a couple other items that the family would want. It smelled very bad, so we just left the windows open and removed the love seat he had died on. (I am saving you some nasty details) The valuables we saved elsewhere.

About a week went by. I had given the Police all the information I had on the man, including a phone number of his mother. A check on the apartment showed that nothing else had been removed. That was strange, because normally family members split up the possessions rather quickly. So, I got on the phone to see what was happening.

I called the number I had and a man answered. "Hi, I'm Charley's landlord," I said, "and I was wondering what to do with his stuff." He responded that I needed to talk with Charley's mother and handed over the phone.

I repeated my question to her and she replied, "Oh, he will be getting paid this week and I am sure he will pay the rent then"! I was jolted into awareness that she knew nothing of his passing! How was I going to get out of this?

"Could I talk with the man who answered the phone?," I asked, as innocently as possible. Instantly suspicious, she asked, "Why, is something wrong with Charles?" After some back and forth, with my asking repeatedly to talk with the man who answered, she became more demanding and suspicious! Since bluntness is one of my dubious virtues, I responded.

"I don't know how to put this gently, but your son has been dead for a week!" I know, I know, believe me, I have rehearsed this conversation a thousand times since, all of them better stated than this. But I was off-guard and unprepared for the SCREAM! It likely peeled the paint off the wall! I heard the phone hit the floor, but the scream continued.

Finally, I did get to talk with the man who first answered and was able to give him some sketchy details. Less than an hour later, Charley's sister was on the phone demanding to know where the rest of his stuff was. They had already plundered what they wanted from the apartment.

But her anguished SCREAM has lingered in my mind for more than 20 years—a mother's greatest fear had come true!

It has been 20-and-counting years of process for me. What I should have said, what I should have done and what to do with it now. Yes, Charley had likely died from a heart attack, very possibly inspired by the ingestion of cocaine. Since he was one of many who die each year in the City, it was just a routine event. Few people know that in many cities the number of homicides and the number of deaths from drug overdoses or reactions is about the same. He had a minimum wage job and was trying to make it on his own. But he was trying to keep his spirits up with a non-prescription solution and paid the price.

Some of the bolder people will ask me why I keep doing stuff in the city, after more than 30 years. I find it hard to tell them all the reasons, particularly this one…Often I hear that scream again in my mind and it pushes me on. Trying to be Jesus is significantly easier with people on their way "UP." We often preach a gospel for Success. But the Gospel is for people on their way down as well. We need to be present with love in any case, and be prepared for the SCREAM.

CHAPTER 7

SECRETS THAT SHOULDN'T BE.

Let's be honest. The roots of the city's problems can be traced back to profit-seeking white males. That is just the history of commerce in America. But, isn't it possible that commercial success carries with it some additional responsibilities?

Consider this statement made by Phil, my accountant. **"It is the responsibility of the rich to be sure the poor have education and opportunity."**

I observe the rich tend to dodge that responsibility in many ways, often inventing new ones when the old ones wear thin. But I suppose the major problem is that the rich are often ignorant of the true state of the poor.

Since When is Ignorance Considered a Virtue?

Let's look again at the general understanding people have of the city. And focus on the size of that understanding first. It is my assertion that few people study cities, though most everyone has an opinion about them. Let's continue with a sports thread. For men, I suspect their primary database has information in the form of trivia from either the NFL, the NHL or MLB. The football teams, the hockey teams and the baseball teams are all connected with that part of the world's geography associated with cities. I won't go into the permutations and combinations that arise from that understanding, I just want to note that it is a very limited view, BUT it means men can learn! If a person can learn and retain sports data, then it should be possible to learn and retain urban data. Let's look at a some of those data fields:

> **HISTORY.** All cities have a history that gives a very good look at the intentions of the city. They have a function that started them, and other functions that keep them going. The change or removal of that function has great effect. The shift of auto manufacturing *out* of the Detroit area has had a great impact, not unlike the demise of the steel industry on Baltimore, Pittsburgh and Gary (Indiana).

POPULATION. Baltimore, like many other rust belt cities, has been depopulating after the creation of the Interstate Highway system. At this point it is home to just over half the people that it was in 1950. Population shifts in terms of ethnicity have happened a couple times. Some Chicago houses and neighborhoods are home to their 4th immigrant group in about 100 years.

NEIGHBORHOODS. Cities are a large collection of small towns in close proximity. Some streets are their own entity, like the "Miracle on 34th Street" a single block in Baltimore's, Hampden neighborhood, which has insane Christmas decorations. Most are more subtle than that. But the more people know about neighborhoods, the better.

CLASS. While the population of Baltimore is majority black, the real estate, particularly downtown is white-controlled. The rich people control the attractions, like the two stadiums, the sports teams, the new casino, the Inner Harbor and the business district. As in most cities, neighborhoods are about class, with racism being a subset of class association.

FUTURE. Each of the represented classes has a view of the future. You might say a hope for the future. With the continuing demise of the working class in our major cities, hope for them is limited. The white professional is trickling back to some areas of Baltimore for reasons of transportation, economy of life, access to attractions and peer pressure.

RACISM. Or rather the response to it. Some cities, like Chicago are still dramatically racist. Most others are more passive, as it has become unfashionable to be racist, homophobic or sexist…or at least to get caught at it. But no city has escaped its effects.

THE POLICE STORY. The hard reality is that there are two kinds of policing in the USA. White and Black. White folk are treated one way, Black folk another. I have talked about this to white folks for years, but was not believed. I claimed that:

- Police often lie on charging documents and reports.
- Police often arrest people without proper cause using flimsy charges which are routinely tossed out of court
- Police often stop people because they are black, search their person and vehicles, require them to sit on the curb or sidewalk like animals *even though* the data does not suggest this is effective.

- Police harm people in custody or while taking them into custody.
- People in the city HATE Police because the Police ARE often criminals by their behavior!
- People can be arrested on false charges, kept in jail because they cannot make bail and then have their charges dismissed months later. No restitution for that.
- White people are routinely given warnings, black people are given tickets.
- Black cops are often HARDER on black people than white cops.
- People can be publicly strip-searched.

This all changed when the Department of Justice did an investigation of the Baltimore City Police Department and found all that and more. This is chronicled in the "Investigation of the Baltimore City Police Department," Civil Rights Division, dated August 10, 2016. City Police Officers were routinely trained to ignore the Constitution and Bill of Rights of the United States and this mistreat the very people they were supposed to protect. This has a huge effect on outreach in the city, because while a church or group needs to respect authority, they are reaching out to people who the system has mistreated. No wonder a couple generations of city children have no respect for the Law or the Church!

Homework Anyone?

Of course there are many more factors to consider, my real point is that **few people do their homework**. Oh, they may study the neighborhood that interests them but few read the dozen or more books that they should as well as have lengthy discussions with knowledgeable people.

Lewis Mumford was a pioneer in the study of cities, writing about them nearly 100 years ago. I was lucky enough to join Baltimore's "Mumford Club" a group that met monthly over breakfast and talked about Baltimore. We also took field trips to Chicago and Pittsburgh before the group faded out. I have yet to discover a similar group. But I think they can be invaluable. Books like "Prairie Metropolis," "Cities without Suburbs, "Baltimore Unbound" and "Black Baltimore" were reading material we discussed.

More recently, a documentary was produced called "Walking While Black," which looks at policing in major cities, Baltimore being a focal point in the aftermath of the Freddie Gray death and subsequent "Uprising." I believe white males, along with others, have some responsibility to educate themselves, being taught by the people who must live with the results.

CHAPTER 8

SECRETS FROM EXPERIENCE:
MICRO CONSIDERATIONS

SECRET 1:
Here is a *Dougatude*:
"*Thoughtful people search for* Insight *and* Perspective."

Insight *is that pivotal cause on a micro level that gives birth to the effect.*
Often the cause of a result is not obvious. Sometimes a small fact can
change everything. The fact that during WW II we could read the Japanese
code was hidden for 50 years. When that became public, it changed the
history books, because that insight trumped the previous conjectures.

Perspective *is the rack that insights are organized upon.* People tend to
form opinions about a city without much of a framework to base it upon,
for example. Baltimore is nearly 200 years older than the town I grew up
near, Sheffield, Iowa, which is a mere 100 years old. That history perspective
is a key to changing my generalizations. Because of racism, black history
struggles for equality. It will take some time for the books to be rewritten
to accurately reflect that. It is my hope that I can add some insights and
perspectives to the understanding of my readers.

**Let me highlight the need to travel to Washington, D.C. to visit the Na-
tional Museum of African American History & Culture.** If you are black,
it will strengthen your legitimate pride in your people. If you are white, it
will strengthen YOUR pride in black people! From the "slave ship" to the
"Mother ship" (sorry, I like Funk, P-Funk, George Clinton, et al,) you will
see the huge impact the black community has had on the USA. I like the
statement on one of the displays on the top floor of that wonderful building next to the Washington Monument, **"God created Black People and
Black People created STYLE!"** Perhaps you know what I mean when that
statement makes you smile knowingly!

Let's put our perspective to work. I am suggesting that Pale Males (and
Females) are not particularly informed or thoughtful about what is going on
in their own city, let alone other ones. Christian Pale Males with a mission,
can be short on understanding, also, perhaps hoping that Bible Study would
overlay their cultural perspectives. But two few have an understanding of
how to relate to city people. Worse, I suspect that many secretly don't care

about their ignorance. They may be able to cite sports trivia at length, but don't know people in the city, nor their stats.

Every minority already knows this.

White men don't get it, (nor do most white women). Logic suggests that since it is so obvious, white folk don't *want* to "get it"…or they would have it; they have the power to do so! It is the core of White Privilege and Social Capital. Whites have the power to ignore all others and they keep that power. In this case, their ignorance gives them strength, because by NOT knowing…means to them they don't have to respond to it. They are often like the gated communities they live in, **if they don't KNOW about the problems of others not inside the fence, they don't HAVE to deal with them.** Blind is one thing, not caring is another. For most white women, they can plead fear and be let off the hook by their race. The women at Dynamic Deliverance love my wife, because few white women want to be in the city and a part of their church either. If she doesn't come with me, which is frequent because of her commitments to our white church, they always ask me to pass on their greetings and best wishes to her. *Always.*

SECRET 2:
At Some Point the *City People* Need to Become *Our People.*

Isaiah 58:9 says, "not to hide yourself from your own flesh." As long as people different from ourselves are held at arm's length, we are not obeying the intent of this verse. We have to move in close and embrace them figuratively if not literally. It is not a simple hurtle to jump.

THE EYES HAVE IT

His blue eyes were watching me carefully. About 2 years old, he had blond hair cut in a "Dutch boy" style, a small straw hat, a homemade blue shirt and a dark jacket with no zippers. He was riding in a shopping cart as his Amish parents were looking for hardware items in a Pennsylvania general store. Yep, he was cute! He seemed not to be familiar with "the English" and stared at me with no fear, just a ton of curiosity. I was only a couple feet away from him, doing my own shopping, when I noticed him. I smiled, returned his gaze and nodded. He didn't smile.

My mind immediately flashed back a few years to a different child, one with dark skin, large brown eyes, tee shirt and shorts. He was staring up at me in the same way, as tho I was the first of my kind he had ever been close to. I was talking to his mother about her delay in paying the rent on her apartment. As we talked, he reached out and took my hand. He stared at the back of it and began rubbing it with his fingers, as tho to see if the "whiteness" would rub off. It suddenly hit me that I was the only white man he had ever touched!

My next thought was that I needed to treat his mother with dignity and respect…which thankfully I had. He had no dislike or hate in his eyes, just curiosity like the Amish boy. I hope it stayed that way over the years…but it will be a struggle. Most likely he would be taught negativity from his encounters with teachers, police, other landlords, the street, employers, stores with bullet-proof glass, and much of his surroundings. But at least it didn't start with me. He could touch me…on a couple levels.

I realized that moment of contact came because I was within touching distance of each of the boys. Had I been further away, we would not have connected. I realized how that simple situation is so typical of ethnicity in the USA.

We are simply not physically close enough to connect.

We don't understand each other because we are too far away and must rely on someone else's stereotype, be it from other adults or from the media.

Some days I feel like condemning people who separate themselves in 'gated communities', because by doing so they remove themselves from the world of the Amish, black kids, Latino kids and others that don't share the majority culture. Worse, some of those people claim to know Jesus. And it makes a major contribution to classism.

I see Jesus moving about with people who are within touching distance. And he noticed. "Who touched me?," his question of the women with the issue of blood. We hope instead that Jesus will touch *us*, ignoring, perhaps, that he wants to touch others through our presence.

A few years back, some college students invited me to join them for a Saturday morning "Bible Club" in East Baltimore. They simply walked through the surrounding city streets knocking on doors asking parents if their children could come that day. Since poor children tend to be house-bound, their tired parents were happy to send them off, without caring much about the church or the program. What really impressed me was all the hugging, patting on the head and eye contact made by the college students to the children. Each hug seemed to be rewarded with a sheepish smile of joy. It was as though most of them were running very low in the hug department! It wasn't just the program that the kids cared about, though they were enthusiastic about it. It was the hugs and encouragement.

You and I are no different. We need to be noticed by Jesus and we need to pass that on to others. The starting point is not the hug but the proximity. I am often asked "how can we help the city?" I reply, "go to a minority church once a month for the next 10 years." White privilege means I don't HAVE to move toward a minority culture, so if I do, it is significant. Because other whites don't. They seem to easily find excuses to do something else…perhaps rearrange their sock drawer.

If we are far away from the ethnic and the needy, we will not be Jesus to them. We cannot share the look, the hand, then hug…in fact we will not even know about it. Perhaps that is the real problem, self-defense rather than self-sacrifice.

And then there was another blue-eyed boy, 11 years old, in 1958. He left school in a great hurry one early spring afternoon, running to get to his nearby church, because **THEY were coming**! He had never seen black people up close, much less a whole choir of them. A white Baptist Pastor from Jackson, MS, took his choir on a fund-raising trip to many churches in Iowa. He drove the ancient bus from breakdown to breakdown, but keep on schedule.

The boy burst into the church where he met the women of the choir, who were setting up cots to sleep on after the concert. He had heard about racial segregation and had learned that black people were not quite on the same level as whites, but didn't know what that meant at the time. They were willing to talk with him and to be friendly even though he didn't really understand them. He had no idea of the fear they had to overcome, the friends and family they left behind or the commitment they had to make to be there. Or the fear they might be turned away from other housing. He just felt their love.

His parents came for him and then returned with him later for the concert. The small church was packed. But there were only 8 women and one of them was playing the piano. How good could they be?

After an introduction, it started. The black pianist grabbed that piano by the keys and give it the thrill of its life! At any given time she seemed to have at least half the keys depressed! They all started singing with a volume that made people in the audience lean back as tho they were trees in the wind......without any kind of sound system. The choir moved, swayed, waved and sang as tho their very life depended on it. The blood shot through the boy's veins and he sat open-mouthed through the performance.

Yes, I was that boy. I remember it as though it was yesterday. It still overwhelms my spirit and brings tears to my eyes. That choir knew something about Jesus and faith that I am still seeking. Even today, as I join the others singing songs most white folks don't know and have never heard about, I am brought to tears...because the Spirit of God comes to me in an overwhelming way.

I cannot remember other details of that event. I wish I could thank each and every one of those 8 women who sacrificed so much ...for me. I wish they knew how God used them in my life and still does 60 years later.

I felt something about them that left me wanting to know more about THEIR God. And that is why we need to connect to the God that is in people who may seem different from us.

SECRET 3:
Here is the *BLOCKBUSTER* I am suggesting. If a pale male or female *DOES* their homework and choses to *BE* among minority city people *WITHOUT* having to dominate, he is highly likely to make a huge difference. If the stubbornness that is his heritage is pressed into service, it can be very useful to the Kingdom of God.

I discovered this by divine accident.

As I got involved with helping a couple growing black churches to acquire buildings and place them in service. I attended over time, but I was careful to simply do what I was asked to do, not think of things for *them* to do. Admittedly, the responses I got from people were confusing. "We see Jesus in you." "When you are here, we feel it." "We miss you when you are not here," "I felt you were coming today." I still get them. Frequently. How could that be? A bit more of my history...

Over perhaps a dozen years, I had built relationships with some *boyz-in-the-hood* but had not seen much change in their lives. I realized that the "street" had more power than I did, because I could not force change in the culture around them. I began to realize that they needed the church much more than I thought and that church needed to be local. They needed a collective of others to give support and being.

So just my "being" with individual guys was not enough to change their lives, but my "being" in a church was enough to ENCOURAGE many. I was not asked to be "in charge" of anything. I was asked to help with a variety of tasks, but not given any positional authority. Which was fine. Interestingly, Bishop Adams and I have major personal commitments to support each other and I am free to do what I see needs doing, but I am not "staff." Somehow my presence was a big deal. More than 10 years later, it still is. I am usually asked to "robe up" when there is a formal graduation ceremony for the in-house Bible training. I stand by my Bishop and shake hands with the recipients. Somehow that is a big deal to folks, my mere presence.

In former years, I believed that if I would let people get to know me, they would see Jesus in me and respond. That seemed to happen with students and military back in the day. But that was also accompanied with lots of Bible study and other kinds of training. I was the "Nav Rep" to my group back at the University of Maryland, College Park. I always suspected that my positional status in the organization was an attraction to some people, but secretly hoped I was right, that the Holy Spirit had been up to something in my life.

I had also been "doggedly at it" for about 20 years when this appreciation of my presence occurred. I wasn't trying very hard to be a "Christian Leader," whatever that was. I spent a big chunk of time as a Landlord, Plumber, HVAC contractor, Salesman, as well as a bunch of street time. I am not particularly inhibited when it comes to language, though no "profanity" is allowed in my role as an Ordained Apostolic Pentecostal Pastor in the Souls for Christ Fellowship. I must switch to my role as a Presbyterian Elder for that! I try to keep up on the street slang and much of that has sexual comment, so sometimes life gets complicated.

I am rambling around to this point: **Remanufactured White Males and Females are the key to city ministry**…in my opinion. The key understanding is that such remanufacturing should produce a firm grasp of BEING over DOING. It is why I am writing this book, truth be told! I am not ruling out minority staff of either sex. I am just saying that Remanufactured white folks can be game-changers…by their PRESENCE, more than their PROBLEM SOLVING! Of course they need to be educated, to study the subject like they were writing a thesis and do the fieldwork worthy of a Ph.D. candidate.

- Know Well the "Secrets" of this Book
- Be on Board the Holy Ghost Train
- Expect to Find Jesus in New Ways and Places.

Ignorance is helpful to no one. But the real ministry is ideally still about relationships and in a church context.

SECRET 4:
FAILURES NEED APPLY: Perfect People Are Not Necessary.

Amy was a computer engineering student at Johns Hopkins, brilliant beyond belief. But she was shy. She signed up to live in one of my apartments on Harlem Ave as a part of one of our summer urban programs in Baltimore City. It was "City" enough that the boyfriend of a friend of hers was forbidden to give her a ride home at night, because the neighborhood was so bad he shouldn't even drive to it…(so they thought)! When Amy and Michelle moved in to my building, I introduced her to Valerie, who lived on the second floor with her two early teen daughters. I had asked Valerie to keep an eye on Amy and her roommate for the summer. When her daughter Jasmine and Amy met, Jasmine said, "Oh, you are shy aren't you" and promptly took Amy under her wing. When the formal program ended in August, Amy spend the next 4 months living alone, the only white girl for blocks around. Everyone knew her on that block and the surrounding ones, and looked out for her, because she needed their help! She graduated from Hopkins the following January, having spent 3 ½ years doing a 4 year program! She recently entered a contest to create a quilt for the Grand Central Station in New York City and won! Not bad for a shy girl!! So having an obvious personality need made her seem real and like the people around her. They would not have believed Amy's starting salary as an engineer!

I would love to get people who have been major failures involved in city ministry. They can be so much easier for people to identify with. Struggling people with a capacity to love others anyway can find a home in city ministry. Weaknesses can be strengths. Humility can go a long ways, Pride can just get off the bus.

My BIG DREAM is that within a couple years, several hundred, then perhaps several thousand white folk (remanufactured of course) will spread out to key cities and attend BLACK CHURCH at least 2 Sundays a month for the next 10 years!!!

That means a bunch of people will need to work at a "**ministry of presence**" in addition to a **ministry of service**. Within the black community, the ministry of presence is understood. Back in the day, when someone died in the community, everyone gathered at the home, with the body in the casket, and was just "there." The times were not necessarily somber, anyone who has attended a "home-going service" knows what I am talking about. There is the time with the casket open and the tears flowing and the shrieks offered. Then the casket is closed and the home-going joy commences. People are present in sorrow and present in JOY! Some of us are a bit stiff, but that wears off over time!

Consider this story:

BURYING BABY

I was asked to officiate at the funeral of a child. He was the size of a young baby, tho he was almost two years old. My Bishop was preaching but didn't want the burden of officiating as well, so I was asked to take that responsibility. Eager to be helpful, I accepted.

Bishop Adams and I had met with the parents and family a couple nights before. The child had been born severely brain damaged because of medical malpractice at a well-known local hospital. From the very start, it was very hard on the parents. One of them needed to watch the child 24-7, because of many seizures, breathing problems and other events, which resulted in many emergency trips to the hospital. In total, the child had spent more than a year, on and off, in the hospital, resulting in astronomical medical bills.

The mother was one of several children of a local minister; the father had recently given up the "thug life" and chosen to follow Christ…tho still carrying the tattoos of his gang involvement. As a part of that commitment to Christ, they were newly married and both working. But with this child, only one could work, so the family income, which was meager, was cut in half. Their relationship was at a breaking point, but they didn't quit.

There was no money to bury the child. I contributed a major sum at the request of my Bishop, who had donated money as well, and who had called in some favors to handle the funeral arrangements. We could buy a plot, get the grave opened and closed, and pay for a small stone…for less that we could just get a grave opened in a white cemetery. I had friends who would donate a plot, but it cost $1,000 just to get it opened!

My eyes were opened as well. I knew that one of the last bastions of racism was in the funeral industry. A black Funeral Director I knew well complained bitterly that he delivered more services than his white counterparts but for much less money. The scene in the old movie, "In the Heat of the Night" flashed to mind as the black Sidney Poitier, as Virgil Tibbs, checked over the rich (but dead) white man's body. White folks don't like the idea of someone who is not white doing the body prep and handling a service. The cemetery we used had long been the final resting place of black folk…and is obscure and somewhat run-down.

The way my black church does funerals is that for about an hour, the casket sits at the front of the church as people pay their last respects. It is seldom a quiet affair. Tears, wailing, screaming and "falling out" are acceptable and understandable…and assisted by women in white dresses armed with Kleenex. Then the immediate family says their last goodbye…and the casket is closed.

It was my job at that point, to step to the podium and explain that we would be moving into the "Homegoing" part of the service, where we would be rejoicing that the loved one was with Jesus. That all sounded fine on paper, but I stepped up just a bit too early and looked down at the casket closing in front of me. **I can't think of a more emotionally charged moment than watching a family close the casket on their baby.** My sense of responsibility trumped my emotions, though just by a whisker. I get tears just trying to write about this.

Yet, this was a moment of joy and relief. The burden of caring for the child was lifted. A year later, the hospital settled the malpractice claim, which re-established the family finances. The parents went back to work and another child came along. But at that moment, people had a choice. Was this the end or just the beginning? We all know people who have figuratively "carried the casket" of a loved one for years. For this family, believed and trusted God, it was not the end. Joy comes in the morning!

While my voice trembled, I explained what we would be doing next and then, thankfully, the band started the introduction for the song we would all sing. The casket was closed, the people of God rejoiced, and hope filled the room. Albeit slowly.

SECRET 5:
Go ahead…ask the question…I know you want to…
What is City Ministry Really and How Do We *Know* We Are Doing It?

Simply put, it is **NET POSITIVE GAIN**. We intersect with people at some point, where they are ready for CHANGE, however small. Starting at that point, we encourage them to progress in their relationship with Jesus, and we join them in the journey. It can look like:

A. A **Pastor** Who Wants to Lead His Church to Disciple Others.
   In black church, there is a major tradition in "doing church." Worship has a particular theme and actions. The idea of 'flight instruction' is not so common (just like white church) Spiritual Reproduction is always a challenge

B. **Repentance** and "Doing Business with God."
   I sat in my "Pastors chair" one New Year's Eve and watched one my 'Deuce Posse" gang members of previous years, sobbing on the steps to the stage as he prayed and repented. He has not been the same since.

C. **Spirit Guidance.**
   I cannot overemphasize that developing a sense of Spirit is important, both inside and outside the church. This journey is not just a mental exercise, but a Spiritual one. Here are the premises behind it:

   1. We are a spiritual people even though some deny it.

   2. We can sense Spirit in others just as the Spirit of God is in us.

   3. It takes a decision to develop this sense of Trust in both yourself and God

D. **Becoming Others Centered.**
   Most people are addicted to something. Addicts are very, very self-centered people. If you attend a Narcotics Anonymous meeting, and I encourage such, you will hear person after person talk about their drug use. If you come back, you will likely hear the same people telling the same stories. Their life is STILL about drugs, but they are not taking them now (or so we hope). At some point, life should move on. They should no longer be defined by a focus on drugs, but a focus on others. People coming home from prison tend to be somewhat shell-shocked by their experience; they need some time before they can look out for others. But they are needed by their communities so preparations need to be made.

E. **Knowledge of the Bible in new ways.**

Don't misunderstand me, I am not advocating Bible ignorance! Living in a Survivalist world is all about stories. It is all verbal, not much written. I am suggesting that a shift be made in how we teach the Bible, to emphasize the story. For example, what are the "Top 10" Old Testament stories? How about the "Top 10" stories told by Jesus? How about the "Top 10" teachings of Paul? And on and on. I don't really care what the stories are, that should be left up to the 'interpretive community' represented. But I am suggesting that disciples should be expected to know specific stories and what they mean. And, of course, live them out.

When most people think "discipling" they think form more than function. A disciple is a "learner" so most are quick to produce a curriculum. Often it can be boiled down to a few key words:

Evangelize — Establish — Equip   *(sound familiar?)*

Which, even the middle class white world actually deals with the:

Spiritual — Emotional — Physical

Generally in that order.

But historically we have selectively focused on only one, or at most two:

Discipling (as done in the 60's, 70's), People could be selected for their minimal problems, with a focus on the Spiritual. Those with too many problems were not selected to the "teams" of my day.

Coaching (done in the 80's, 90's), A little looser training, more background given, and the emotional needs engaged as well as the spiritual.

Mentoring like a Flight Instructor –(currently, particularly poor and urban). The *discipler* must engage the physical needs (housing, food, safety) as well as the emotional and spiritual, so the hierarchy of needs are reversed. Yet, the trust in a mentor is limited while the job is a large one. Trust is not easy to obtain in the city.

The key for city people is that even while discipling looks more like mentoring, the people are still making **Net Positive Gain**. And the staff or volunteer person, the person capable of mentoring, needs to be qualified to mentor in all Three…Spiritual, Emotional, Physical.

Oh, the concept of Net Positive Gain is a simple one, yet at the very heart of discipling. It simply says that we help people starting where they are. And then help them move toward Jesus. The change in them over time is Net Positive Gain. It contrasts with having a cultural-based system of standards that everyone is expected to conform to within a specific period of time.

Measurement (to determine Net Positive Gain) is simply taking people where they are now, subtracting where they were and Praising God for the difference!!! It is expected that individuals in training will be a part of someone's intentional plan. In that sense, everyone can benefit from a "special education" plan called an "IEP," or Individual Education Plan." Setting up a pattern for all is not so necessary, the IEP can simply be looking at what the next steps might be for an individual and writing them down. Or agreeing to them verbally.

Can you really disciple, coach or mentor someone you really don't know? Doubtful.

Are there levels of understanding to consider? Yes, we will deal with that a bit later.

Sooner or later, the person fails in some way. *What then?*

F. Tomorrow Is Another Day…Forgiveness "For Real."
For many years, a diminutive nun ran an after school program for poor urban kids at the Julie Center in East Baltimore. Troubled kids would come there to receive hugs and encouragement from her when they came, left and in between! And so did I on occasion!! Her name is Sister Roberta English, but everyone knew her as Bobby, or Sister Bob! She has spent her entire life working with the poor, both in Chile and Baltimore. I loved talking with her, she was incredible. The Baltimore Sun newspaper described her as, "Looks like 50, acts like 30 but is really 70." I asked her how she dealt with the problem kids, and she said, "They must behave or I put them out. But tomorrow is a new day." In other words, if you got thrown out, you could come back tomorrow as though you had never "sinned." She was so loving that no one wanted to be separated from her love. That and other ideas were a great blessing to me. I *want* to be forgiven and have a new day tomorrow, but sometimes I find it hard to extend that to others. We need more people like Sister Bob.

Forgiveness is available for you as well. Mistakes with confession and remorse can result in forgiveness, reconciliation and restoration. Much is forgivable in the black community. But perhaps you should not wear them out with continual ignorance!

We all get wounded because we all have vulnerabilities. What happens then? If we are physically wounded, we apply anti-germ substance and cover it with a bandage. So how do we treat the internal wounds to our spirit? Wounds to the soul and spirit are vulnerable to an infection called bitterness. The symptom is frequently tears or anger. Untreated, it festers and becomes septic, causing damage to our whole body. The oozing bitterness can block spiritual growth, servant hood and fellowship with others. The polar opposite of the "Fruit of the Spirit," highlighted in Galatians 5:22, can be observed!

But if you put a little Forgiveness on a wound as soon as possible, it helps the healing process.

If you put more Forgiveness on the scabs that cover a wound, it softens it up.

If you put more Forgiveness on the scar, it can help shrink it.

CHAPTER 9

UNCOVERING SEX IN THE CITY

I want to talk about love, sex and drugs. You WILL encounter that triumvirate, so even tho many Christian writers might look the other way, I think we need to go there. I hope to educate a bit and perhaps attack a myth/stereotype that black people are genetically oversexed. For centuries, white folks have wondered, perhaps fantasized, about sexuality in the black world. Many times young whites have come to the black community to "see if it was so," that black people offered special sexual pleasure. Perhaps this discussion will take some of the edge off that notion.

I would note that all three, **love, sex and drugs** exist everywhere in the USA including the closed societies like the Amish, Mormons and others. And no culture seems to escape. However, particularly among the Survivalists, there are some variations.

By the way, none of us have unlimited capacity for loving others. We all have our limits. It is very critical, particularly when the ministry is all about giving away one's self, to keep tabs on the level in your "love tank." You cannot give away what you do not have without damaging yourself in some way. Usually by leaning too much on the people that have needs themselves. So the starting point is internal, not external. You cannot give what you have not acknowledged receiving. You cannot fill your tank by stealing it from others.

First Love. Most of us experience love from our parents right from the start. Since we can give little back in the early years, we simply suck it in. However, where there is LIMITED love available, love can become a transaction. Parents in SOME urban settings have a very limited amount of love to give away. Like everyone else, they give the first shot to their kids.

However, ADDICTION robs that love, making the **primary affection the addiction**. This is visible in Suburbia as well when the parents spend many hours out of the house and leave the kids in the hands of others. I sometimes think a job and a career have every bit as much to do with addiction as do the opiates. But early on, kids learn they must compete with something to get attention, affection and love. Some friends of mine work with some at-risk kids who are in a private grade school. Those kids have been allowed to grow up mostly unsupervised, unguided and undisciplined. Whatever pops into their little heads, they do. They don't know where their next meal is coming from, when they will get to bed or even where they will find a bed. So they "act out," they seek attention by misbehaving. They don't believe that people really love them or that they can love back. A lack of love has made them very difficult to teach, control or even to love.

My grandchildren receive lots of love and it shows. How? Because they can give love. They will smile and hug me, not because they want something, but because they appreciate me. And they have kisses and hugs to give out. They are experiencing an abundance of love everywhere in their environment. Not so much with some of the city kids.

Fast forward a few years. **Survivalist kids learn about sex very early**. Since toddler days, they have watched adults and teens indulge themselves in sex play. They have watched early teens get pregnant and have played with the babies. They have likely had sexual advances made to them at an early age. Some of it they liked, some of it they hated. But they learned early to **manipulate** by denying a response or by giving one… without love being involved. Or at least the kind of love that doesn't expect something in exchange.

There is an old adage, "**Women give sex to get love, Men give love to get sex**" . There is some truth to that, but the question is what does love really look like? There is an old Rock Song which comments, "you get the maximum pleasure from the minimum love" (Mac MacAnally, "Minimum Love") So the challenge is to give up the least amount of yourself in exchange for the maximum pleasure. Or so it would seem.

That can translate into difficult living situations in the city. The man doesn't bring home much money, but he brings security and warmth on a cold night. The cost to the woman is to let him have sex. In exchange, the man protects the house and is fed. But love may not have much to do with it, once the passion is expended. The clever man SAYS that love has something to do with it, but maybe not. Sex, food and a warm place to sleep mean a lot to a Survivalist. He is committed to her until the next possibility comes along…and he gets caught with her!

"What's Love Got to Do With it?" asks Tina Turner. "What's love but a second-hand emotion?" I guess it depends on what you have experienced.

But if you ask any urban mom about her kids, she loves them as much as she can. In many ways, they are all she has and perhaps all she will have. Yes, they may have different fathers, but perhaps that says more about men in the city than it does the women. They love their children and grandchildren……as best they can, however they came into being.

Since love may be a bit thin between men and women, or any urban couple, there is a strong temptation to "love" by domination or control. Particularly if their experience has been being dominated or controlled. City sex culture can inspire young men to be sexually active early. Making women into objects to be used and abused is frequent for street life. All the more reason to deal with respect and dignity.

Sex is much less hidden in the city. Even in church. A pastor friend told me, "When I was growing up, my mother tried to protect the girls from me. When I became a pastor, she tried to protect me from the women!" There is a certain desperation to desired relationships, to pursue and to conquer and share the spoils. I am suggesting it is on both sides.

Sex is readily available, particularly oral sex. And it is not expensive. I could get more graphic here, but what I am mainly trying to do is to prepare people for what they are likely to experience. Prostitution is rampant... fueled by drugs.

She Needed a Ride

I had spent plenty of time in and around the street culture before I met her. I was familiar with the actions and activities of prostitution in the parts of the city I was doing my landlording. To be honest, the street hookers were not particularly attractive, nor were they subtle. When she approached, looking like an attractive college student, I had no defenses up.

"I missed my bus but I need to get home and I don't have enough money," was her opening line. I was pumping gas at North and Madison. She was young, dressed well and didn't seem to be high. She did claim to be a college student from nearby Coppin State.

"Where is home?" I asked. She described it and it was in the direction I was headed.

"I can give you a ride," I offered innocently.

We chatted as I drove off, getting to know each other a bit. For some reason, I felt compelled to mention I was a minister with a wife and family. After a while, she commented, "I do need some money," she volunteered. I didn't particularly catch on at the time. She clarified, "I need $20 and I don't mind doing something for it. Something that will make you feel good. You don't have to tell your wife." I did know what she meant, an oral sex act. But it caught me by surprise.

"What do you need the money for?" I asked, still a bit clueless.

"Ok, you seem like a nice guy, let me be honest with you. I am feeling sick and I need some medicine." This was code for needing a hit of heroin.

I did recognize that.

"Sorry, I am a Christian and I don't feel comfortable giving you money for drugs." I responded. "And I am not looking to cheat on my wife."

"She wouldn't have to know and what I can do for you will only take a minute," she replied.

"Sorry, I have to say no. I just can't give you any money." I said.

She lapsed into silence as we drove into her apartment complex. She made one more ploy.

"You know I will have to get that money somewhere and they might not be as nice as you. So why can't you help me out?"

"Sorry, this is where you get out," I replied. I watched her walk slowly in the direction of what she claimed was her apartment.

Two lessons to highlight from the experience. First, drugs will drive people to do most anything. Men or women. Second, I had decided what I would do in that situation ... **before it happened**. And it paid off. Sexuality has the power to wipe out good sense once the situation presents itself. For men, certain views of certain parts of the human body will trigger a response that skips right over logic! Perhaps a variation of that is true for women as well.

It reminds me of the first parachute jump I made in the U.S. Army Airborne. I had spent two weeks of boring practice, jumping out of towers and practicing hitting the ground correctly. But when the command came in the aircraft to "STAND UP" then "HOOK UP" then "EQUIPMENT CHECK" then "SOUND OFF FOR EQUIPMENT CHECK" finally, "STAND IN THE DOOR"; the drama and challenge of the moment blocked my ability to think. The next thing I knew, the Jumpmaster yelled "GO!" in my ear and I was falling through the air. When my chute opened and I was floating down, my senses began to return to normal. All that practice I had complained about suddenly came in handy. **I had done what I rehearsed not what I could think about at the time.**

I once asked a man who had hopped into bed with a married woman, whose husband was in jail, and then she got pregnant by him, "What were you thinking?." The answer was simple, **HE WASN'T**! So I am suggesting that to be unprepared is to be vulnerable. To be unrehearsed is dangerous, particularly on the street.

It is not talked about much in the media, but certain illegal drugs make the sexual experience longer and more pleasurable. So if a man has those drugs, he can find partners to share them...and the sexual experience. You can get high AND have sex last a long time. It can be boring to be a survivalist and to be poor. So marathon sex can be very desirable. Don't forget, women like to get high too!

Therefore, it can become a circular trap; **drugs, sex, transactional love**… then move on. "Baby Mama Drama" is a direct result from such activities. I recall a day laborer who worked for my buddy's plumbing company. He wanted to be paid every 4 hours, or at least get an advance at noon. Somehow his women would find out where he was working and stop by to get money for Pampers or other necessities, at noon! He had babies by several women and there was a major competition for his paycheck.

If you are a woman without money, what do you do if you need drugs bad? What might seem easy when you are desperate is to offer oral sex on the street or in a car. The going rate is about the same as the price of a drug dose ($20) and it might not seem that difficult…after the first few times. Particularly if you are high on heroin. Granted, this is not a self-esteem building exercise!

Likewise if you are a struggling woman with children and someone does something very kind for you? Since you think you have nothing else, perhaps a small sex act in a parking lot is a way to repay that kindness. Or a larger time in a room somewhere. It makes sense on one level, but can wreck many relationships on another. Being well-treated with kindness & respect in a society of transactional love can inspire a sense of needing to repay, but there is no money, so…

A lot of what I am trying to suggest here is that sex can be very open on the streets, and thus in the church as well. That same little girl or boy who was "acting out" in grade school may not have matured much more socially, and is willing to bargain physically and emotionally. To work and relate in the city one should be prepared.

My observation is that there are a couple traps for the unsuspecting. First, **people who are needy may not be helpless!** Many a man has begun by helping a woman with a chore only to be repaid by sex of some sort. Many a man gets wrapped up in a woman's troubles and becomes sexually involved because his own desires have been hidden from himself. Sex can also be about greed, anger, resentment, jealousy and domination. Those can be repressed, but come to the surface when hormones, sex drive and opportunity present. By the time you are "helping" them out of their underwear, it may be too late!

It can also be about hidden fantasy. We don't know each other's secret thoughts, so that nice Godly person who talks about "missions to the poor" may harbor secret desires about cross-racial sex. He has his fantasy, she has her fantasy (or needs) and they discover they can fulfill each other's dream.

A combustible situation. The boundaries that are present outside the city may not be as obvious IN the city, and sexual liaisons occur between otherwise "fine, Christian people." **So be sure someone you know and trust knows your secrets**. Or the whole world may know eventually!

Control And Domination

I think it is fair to say that Intentionalists are all about control. They live under the myth that with just a bit more effort, they can control their lives, dodging danger, limiting the variables, being right all the time, and being sure others accomplish goals that are important to the Intentionalist. Of all myths, the myth of human control may be the worst and most deceptive.

"Control" has a partner on the street and elsewhere called "Domination." **The Intentionalist AND the Survivalist** both work to control their relationships. Which CAN mean it is all about controlling people. It might be the church leader who has a beautiful but weak (from his point of view) daughter and he tries to keep her from running amok. Using his cell phone, he can track her by GPS, require frequent texts as to her actions, screen her friends via social media and withhold his approval. The street drug gang also works to control the actions of its "members." Assignments are given as absolutes, under the penalty of death. Often sex is a part of the control. Women are lured into addiction and then become sex slaves under control of the gang and kept there by drug habits.

Those who would dominate and make illegitimate requests of the other, may tell themselves they have the best of intentions, from the overbearing father to the gang leader, to the abusing spouse to the youth pastor. The desire for "the best" of another person, or the desire to actually "have" all the other person has, from personality to sexuality, can be extremely strong. For the heteros, it may be easier to see domination in same-sex relationships. In a prison culture, the rules may be somewhat different, but it is domination and control just the same. The inmate who returns to his cell and finds a "Little Debbie" pastry on his bed, has just received notice that he "belongs" to someone...like it or not!

Some people think they can get a life by sucking the life out of someone else! That makes them a predator. But it also means they don't trust God and are not likely to trust you for a period of time. But the neediness of others can be a deep well, a minefield, a trap for the foolish. Don't go there without a safety line......

I think it is important to note that the average well-intentioned person is not prepared to properly help people caught up in control and domination. Leave that to the professionals. Even relationships with the two-people involved can be quite difficult, so when this is encountered, **SEEK HELP**!

If you read this and are either the victim or the perpetrator of a co-dependent, domination and control situation, you will also need professional help.

I observe that it is common to underestimate the power of one individual over another. Some years ago, my son was running a cash register at a gas station, when a "money changer" came in. It began with a "can you change a 20" and a few changes later, using increasing bills, the customer left. He had outsmarted my bright son out of about $50. The lesson he learned was that people who are manipulators are powerful people. The Con Man plays to the expectations of others by telling them what they want to hear. On the street, the needy 14 year old girl can be as dangerous as a cobra to the untrained male. Ditto for the homeless man, the street preacher and the poor woman with a handful of kids. Kind-hearted people are easy marks for the con artist, sexual manipulator and dominator. Their stated mission may be one thing, but their actions bespeak of another.

The Failures

It is not uncommon for the boundaries and rules of one culture to be undone in another. Another reason to not have intentions to be a "Hero of the Faith," but rather a part of a community.

I would note that in general the black church shows much more good sense about dealing with sexual misconduct than the white church. For some reason, a moral failure on the part of white Christian leaders is usually treated as a terminal disease. Once accused, the wrath of the church descends upon them, often in unkind ways. No so much in black church. The pastor who strays is asked to "sit down" for a period while he and his family heals. He is encouraged by friends and given professional help if needed. Then, he returns to service, to restoration.

In my opinion, critical to that return is the **lessons learned**. It is true that some leaders simply deny that anything bad happened. To them, it is the other person's fault. Not acceptable. **Moral failure has to go back to some failure to trust God.** It is not enough to simply confess; the root cause must be dealt with and a new vision developed.

A former mentor had a great concept. **"Never Fail Alone, Never succeed Alone."** I have a great relationship with my Bishop at Dynamic Deliverance Cathedral. I trust him with my inner life, I believe he trusts me with his. We review situations we find ourselves in and defuse them with reality. Somehow when one attaches a timeline to a problem relationship, it becomes clear that crossing certain lines will not be worth it. Having to explain your twisted thoughts to someone helps a great deal in seeing the folly of the path…particularly with an honest risk/reward analyses.

I think the big key here is to understand the situation on the street.

Then be sure you understand yourself.

Then have someone who you can trust to be accountable with your realities.

Then learn to understand the struggles of sexuality for other people.

Judging them is not particularly helpful here… So plan to do some growing and understanding.

,

Chapter 10

What Should be learned?

A Thoughtful Trainee Might Ask, **"I Have a Passion for the City, What Should I Expect to Learn?"**

People Are Not Always What They Seem.

I watched a frequent panhandler on the city-county border street recently doing a "heroin nod" one Sunday as I drove to church. To the untrained, it just looked like he was napping. I wonder how many people knew that the money they were donating was going to his habit. Learning to "see" who people are is key to ministry with them. I began my efforts in the City of Baltimore by hating "drug pushers." It turned out that they didn't push at all. The people *wanted* the drugs! Most of the people I connected with sold drugs at some point in time or used drugs at some point in time. At my age, every morning I take my meds. So do the city people, they just don't bother the pharmacist!

You Must Know Your City.

One of the first questions I ask when I meet people from Baltimore is "where do you live"? I ask for a street and cross-street. About 90% of the time I can remember enough about the area they reference to make a connection with a local landmark, store, people or event and *presto*, we are talking like we have known each other for some time. The quicker people know their city, the more it shows in their talking. Jump in the car with, me or other city veterans. We can drive all over the place without a map while telling stories. "Rookies" can't do that.

You Must Learn to be Comfortable on the Street.

That is demonstrated by how you stand, how you gesture, and what you notice. There is a lot to how comfort is developed, more than I can describe here. Urban folk can read the comfort level of people at some distance. They can see it in how people move and see it in their eyes. You will be tested, like the time I watched a large cockroach jump off the sick person's bed and onto my bare leg. I didn't bat an eye, just nudged him off my leg and stepped on him with a crunch. The person I was visiting didn't even know and I didn't want to embarrass him.

You Must Learn to Have Different Expectations.

You will recognize the new ones when they come. Some of the old ones will burn on contact, others will die slowly. In any case, it is frustrating. I started out hating drug dealers. Then I understood they were secretly wanted by many in the community and had connections there. I needed to let the Police do their job and I needed to do mine. I learned that virtually everyone has a drug problem and that is why there are dealers around. To fight drugs is to fight the very people I want to help. Again, many lines can get blurry.

You Must Learn to Be Comfortable With Chaos, Mess, and Disorganization.

Not to mention the sights, sounds and smells. It can be the sounds and smells that push one over the edge. Poor houses have a lot of all three. Learning to sit and relax amid the folk may require clenched teeth at first!

You Must Learn to Build Strange Relationships.

At one point I was part of a "gang," four young black men and myself. We named ourselves, "The Deuce Posse" (I don't know why!) They had addictions to heroin, I didn't. I was old and white. They weren't. That was 20 years ago and we are still in touch. Two of them are clean and trying to walk with Jesus. We found that attending ANY church together was hard on the regular attenders. Most churches talk about outreach but don't really plan to do it. And we were a scruffy bunch to show up in ANY church!

You Must Learn to Be Comfortable Having Race Discussions.

White folk rarely discuss racism, black folk discuss it all the time. If you are a "safe" white person, you should expect to hear stories, indignation and pain. It is the pain that is the deep secret to racism. Like a knife wound that can be done slowly or quickly like a paper cut, it causes indefensible pain.

Most black people experience race pain somewhat frequently. Few whites have a clue. To them, racism is a mental exercise. They don't understand that *discrimination causes pain!* To share that pain is to build relationships. But any race-inspired pain can result in everything from tears to anger.

Plan to share it and to do some processing.

Make no suggestions.

Just feel their pain.

You Must Believe that Your Faith Will Show Your Spirit.

And that it is a good thing. Let people see who you are and they can believe what you believe. As a Pastor, I can wear a black suit and cleric collar on the streets. I can easily have conversations, because people know what I stand for. The collar makes it easy for people to know who I am. I can also do that in shorts and tee shirt, if I identify with a nearby church. But people also respond to the Spirit they sense in me. They seem to sense I care and I have worked to understand them.

You Will Need to Appreciate the Local Ethnic Church.

For example here is my **Top Ten things to appreciate about black church:**

1) **Lots of flexibility of worship styles and response**. At any given time, worshipers can be everything from asleep to running up and down the aisles. The platform leadership and the band are very keyed to the working of the Holy Ghost in the people who are present.

2) **Strong sense of Spirit**; from God to his people and to each other.

3) **Strong sense of the other person's struggles and joys**. Weeping and shouting in response to the sorrows and joys of others

4) **Worship is FELT**. In the enthusiasm of the people, the impact of the music and the delivery of the message. White folk often expect Mental challenge from a sermon, good black preachers also deliver FEELING with their thoughts. BTW, wherever did we get the notion that worship is NOT felt?

5) **Skilled support staff from the platform Nurse to the Usher Board**. They easily handle the intoxicated on one hand and the "slain in the Spirit" on the other. Worshipers are free to "let go," knowing they will be attended to not stared at. In fact, they will be supported and cared for.

6) **An expectation that Jesus will show up!!** In many white churches, there seems to be little expectation that worship is more than an intellectual exercise. No possibility of the Holy Ghost being free to work.

7) **Respect for the Pastor and others in authority**. A person may be a nobody at work during the week, but their spiritual service makes them somebody on Sunday. Titles define ministry responsibilities and identify their place in the Kingdom.

8) **Celebration of a cultural perspective**. I cannot overemphasize this. After 14 years, I still get blessed in new ways EVERY Sunday. It often feels like a dive into a swimming pool!

9) **A place where people find not only forgiveness and reconciliation, but restoration for those who want it.** In the white Christian world, failure is often forever. Forgiveness comes sometimes, reconciliation occasionally and restoration very seldom. Not so in most black churches. Failure is NOT forever.

10) **An appreciation of visitors**. Visiting from other churches is a much more common experience in black church. It is common for them to announce greetings from their other church. Visiting clergy are often invited to the platform and given the opportunity for a "Word." It is perfectly acceptable to "bring greetings from your home church."

And of course, there is more that could be added to this list.

I want to give a further example of what kinds of things city rookies need to process. It can be surprising to discover all the things that we chafe at.

QUIRKS OF THE URBAN POOR...
That May Bother White Folks

- **They don't always buy the cheapest.** In part, this is due to the tendency to buy at the nearest store because they have no transportation. But also due to knowing name brands and being suspicious of generics.

- **They watch a lot of TV.** Most houses have multiple TV's that are on nearly 24/7. In contrast, many of the wealthy people I know have only 1 or 2 and they are never left on.

- **They don't have many clocks or watches** and don't give time a lot of thought. I know of no poor men who wear watches.

- I have never heard a poor woman say that she had more children to **increase her welfare check**. While the reasons vary, I think the core of it is the same for all of us, we want to leave a legacy and hope that legacy will love us when others will not.

- **The poor travel very little beyond their city.**

- **The poor don't take vacations!!**

- **The poor have few books…since they don't read well, they watch TV**. Of course, since they watch TV they don't read!

- Generally, **the poor don't do a lot of planning** because they lack the resources, including Social Capital, to do anything anyway. Plus their plans always seem to fail.

- Generally, the **poor live in the moment**…it may be their last!! 1 in 8 black men in Baltimore will be shot in their lifetime.

- **Sheets are a luxury**; many poor just sleep on the mattress.

- Many poor do **their laundry in the bathtub using hand soap, hence no sheets.**

- **Smoking** a cigarette is a luxurious moment for many people. That hit of drugs, booze or whatever can likewise **be beyond luxurious**. There is a reason why people do it, it makes sense to them. If you understand that, and can understand how that makes sense, then you are on the way to feeling at home in the city.

- **Somebody knows**. Everyone in the 'hood knows where people are at all times. They are always watching. You may remember the story of Amy, the white girl who lived on Harlem Ave. Some of her friends went to pick her up one day but she was not at her apartment. In a panic, they called me, secretly assuming something bad had happened to her. I told them to just stop the next person they saw and ask them. "Oh, the white girl went around the corner to the store," they were told. Sure enough, Amy came around the corner just then. The street is a large stage, be sure you know your part.

- **Stay loose**! Remember Relentless? It never sleeps but keeps secrets until something breaks them loose. We use the term, "jump off" as is "Something might Jump Off." It simply means that one should expect the unexpected and that careful planning is a waste of time. Plan in general, of course. Plan in great detail…maybe a waste.

- **Different is not wrong**. This is a general advice when crossing cultures, life is easier if you don't begin by assuming your way is the only way. A variation of this is **"He doesn't have to wrong for me to be right."** That is a way of saying you don't need to make someone else be wrong to justify what you are doing. Christianity has plenty of paradoxes we can't explain, so two people CAN have totally opposite understandings and both be right.

And there are more to add to this type of list. Let me know your favorites.

And There are Some Things to DO!

Develop skill in USING TOOLS.

In the service industry, the use of tools is critical. I have adapted several techniques in repairing complex water heaters that make my job much easier and quicker. I am always searching for better and lighter tools for my tool bag. So what tools are needed for the urban worker? I have referred to some previously, but here is a slightly different perspective.

Geography. When I was learning the streets of Baltimore, I often studied maps until I had them memorized. Whenever possible, I take a different route to get to my destination. My brain has Google Earth type pictures of certain places. One simply MUST know the city.

History. From street names to monuments, cities have a history. From Francis Scott Key to Theodore McKeldon to the Shot Tower to the Falls Road Mills…and beyond, there is a history that has affected its residents. One should be always learning more.

Conversational skills. From the PoPo knockers (plainclothes police who do 'jump-outs' and slam people against buildings) to the "Kitchen Zinc, (sink) Hon," Baltimore has slang expressions. Listening and understanding them is critical to the comfort of your new acquaintants. Street expressions can be both profane and sublime!!

Language skills differs a bit in that street language varies. There is a street level of profanity that one may chose not to use, but learning the inflections and nuances in case there is a need to use them is important. During a visit to Jamaica, I heard an angry Jamaican use the term "blood clot." Turns out it is the vilest and disgusting name possible to call someone. It meant nothing to me, but had I used it in casual conversation around Jamaicans, I would have paid for my ignorance! The term, "OH, Jesus" can be either praise or profanity…depends on the usage! So learn the language and learn when to use the words that give you cred.

Knowing What NOT to do can also be quite helpful. Here are some examples. I discovered early on that PERSONAL questions are to be used carefully. Street names are used, but not personal names. For example, I don't know Killer's real name. I don't ask questions about family structure. Very few marriages on the street level, so asking "who is your wife" or the like will result in some suppression of the discussion. "Do you have kids?" … is acceptable, but may not be easy to keep track of. Also, some terms may be hard to grasp like, "My sister's Father," or "my girlfriend's husband" (!). Also, avoid certain kinds of arguments. Anything that attacks an ego is to be avoided. Most people have little ego strength, *(remember dignity and respect?)*

so disrespect can authorize the use of nuclear warheads. Or send bullets your way. But apologies can be a sign of weakness, so you may have to discuss loudly (without insult) to get respect. I find that simple raising my voice and speaking clearly and concisely gets me heard.

Checkpoints of cultural immersion. How do you know you are making progress?

- ❑ Being told "secrets" like cultural quirks and confidences
- ❑ Understanding and appreciating the various aspects of the culture.
- ❑ Knowing the streets and being comfortable on them.
- ❑ Knowing significant people in the neighborhood and beyond.
- ❑ Sharing the pain of racism and discrimination.
- ❑ Knowing the word clues. "Kin I get a Mix, Miss?" the words to use to order a half-iced tea, half-lemonade from a black vendor at the corner carry-out.
- ❑ Knowing the players at a glance.

Knowing what cultural shackles may be present.

- Like Plantation Psychosis. This is the need for a minority to have majority approval. For some black people, they will not attempt something without white approval. They are powerless in the meantime. Also, there must be white affirmation for the effort to be ongoing. This is never admitted, of course, but observation will give clues. Interaction with people employed in a bureaucracy can be instructive. This becomes a shackle in two ways… One is that some black churches try very hard to win white approval, often by being in a white-controlled denomination. The second is the opposite, that a few churches go out of their way to avoid being friendly to white folks. I think it is important to give affirmation as a white person rather lavishly, regardless of culture. And be quick to be submissive to the decisions of the cultural leadership.

- Like always being the target of panhandlers. I can see the look in their eyes a block away. They are going to ask for money and I will tell them NO.

- And there is always the scam artist. That can be an expensive education, but since it is usually individual, you are on your own. Just be sure to have a partner or companion who has good sense.

A willingness to BE Jesus! We have all seen the WWJD bumper sticker, (What Would Jesus DO?,) a distinctly white view. I would change it to WWJB, (What Would Jesus BE)? The notion of a "ministry of Presence" is part of black tradition. When a slave would die, the body was placed in the house, not unlike "sitting shivas" in the Jewish community, and the family and friends would gather to be in the presence of the body but also each other. Talking was not necessary, just the presence of each person was itself a gift. When I was an inner-city landlord, I worked at just that. I noticed that it was the Jewish folks who were the majority landlords and I also noticed the care they had for their tenants. I also noticed the lack of Christians in that business. Why? Because it is tough! I probably evicted over 75 people during my 10 years as a landlord. Each time I tried to be Christlike. Not easy. But none of the people I knew who rented from me was a candidate for homeownership. It was simply more than they could manage. Making people homeless is not exactly a ticket to affirmation, but I did get positive feedback from many former tenants in the form of greetings later.

Chapter 11

Secrets of Engagement

Many people like to take the Bible literally and just "preach the word, in season and out." Whether they think about it or not, the presumption is that people only lack a **small amount of information**. Upon being told that information, people will pray and trust Jesus, thus insuring their Eternity. Is that really the situation? Are people who have been ignored, oppressed, and ignored some more...... likely to believe the next white person who comes along? Has that been your experience?

I am convinced that we live in a "Misinformation" society. We have all kinds of information at our fingertips via "smart phones," Google and the rest of the Internet. However, we have also then rejected the need to mentally retain data and to think about it.

I like the wisdom I saw on a TEE Shirt,

> **"There is no such thing as THE CLOUD.**
> **It is just someone else's computer!"**

How is that for truth and clarity? In reality, we are fed a steady diet of questionably irrelevant data and no perspective to hang it on (Remember that wise people look for INSIGHT AND PERSPECTIVE?) What it has fostered is a lack of trust in information. We have mountains of data but piles of skepticism to climb over when we get there.

Perhaps now, more than ever before, simply quoting a Bible reference isn't enough. It has to have some real life attached to it.

My experience is that people on the street DO indeed have a spiritual sense. We commonly send college students out on the "mean streets of Baltimore" in two's and tell them to simply stop people and ask if the students can pray for them. It is very rare that they are refused! They don't lack information, they lack trust. What good is a Gospel that doesn't really listen to them? They usually know the Gospel, they just don't believe that it is a reality *for them*!

We do indeed "hold the truth in earthen vessels." But are we to dump that Truth over people's heads like the "Ice Bucket Challenge" or is it administered like a "cup of cold water" on a hot day?

I like the notion that we are to "scratch where people itch." Somehow we want to *listen* to people and **join them in THEIR discovery of God**, not just pass out information. Granted, for many people, their lives are a huge mess, at least by our standards. I would suggest we are not there to provide *solutions* to their problems but rather to stand with them as they try to address an unbearable ITCH!

How skilled are you in relationships? More than a little be introverted? Remember the story of Amy, back in chapter 5? Actually, introversion may be more helpful than extroversion. It will let you be more of a student and to keep listening as a priority. But first, you may need so ideas and some details about building relationships and developing them across race and class lines.

So here are some "**jumpin' in**" secrets.

First, I am taking you back to my 7 Stages that I mentioned in Chapter 1.

My Seven Stages

1. Seeing People as Objects...

2. Feeling Sorry for Certain People

3. Getting a Desire to Actually Know Certain Groups of People

4. Having a Desire to BE Like Them

5. Having the Desire to BE WITH Them

6. Hanging My Heart There

7. Never Wanting to Leave

What stage are you are on?

If you are on stage 1,2 or 3, then look for a program, a plan or an opportunity to serve. You simply need time and experience. Go to Black Church. Or a minority Church that you chose.

If you are on stage 4 or 5, you may be ready to pursue more efforts ahead of your peers. You will need some deeper relationships over time, so study, connect, relate, enjoy.

If you are on stage 6 or 7, you just need to hear from people like me, "Welcome Aboard!"

By the way, one test of all this is in how you connect with the ugly people. Yes, I used that word. Those with horribly distorted bodies, minds or attitudes. What do you see? Do you look for their ASSETS or just kindly and nicely hold them at arm's length? How quickly can you see past the ugly? And sense the golden, to see what God sees? If they are YOUR people (however you want to define it) you will work at such insight. Pity is not sensitivity. It is just your emotions. The blessing comes when you appreciate what God appreciates.

Consider the Concept of "ENGAGEMENT"

Think of the meshing of gears. Or releasing the clutch. Or putting the shift lever into DRIVE!

It doesn't matter if you decide to make some friends on a block in your city or go to a church to make your start. The connections are made the same way. You must meet people.

However, if you just "jump in" to a street setting, the major question you must demonstrate and answer for is **"What are you doing here?** Each city block in high density areas is like a stage. Every day, characters move across that stage in different roles. What will your role be? I can't answer that for you. I have been a landlord, plumber, contractor, real estate investor, employer, Pastor and friend.

Perhaps the **easiest connection is with a local church**. In my case, I can put on a Clergy collar and talk to all kinds of people about spirituality very easily; identifying as a Pastor. They all know what that role is. And are pleasantly surprised they can talk to me; or rather that I will listen to them. We frequently wear "Dynamic Deliverance Cathedral" TEE shirts, which also say **"Come and get your Deliverance! How bad do you want it?"** … the message is right up front! But there is no doubt who we are and what we are about. And that does not scare city people.

Giveaways and Interactives kick in here and become much more effective. I am not a fan of the long reach from suburbia, but under the umbrella of a local church, they fit in. Reality is that there are really needy people in parts of the city that are not being connected. The church can respond out of friendship and love for the community, not pity or shame. At Dynamic Deliverance, we do most of the **Giveaways and Interactives** on a small, sensible basis. Those activities just seem to fit right in and don't require a ton of programming.

It is about the "Process"

As I use my experiences and look both backward and project forward, it seems to me there are levels of relationship that define and direct.

We all have contacts, **acquaintances** and friends. The longer you stay in one place, the more people on the list. I have lived in the same house for 35 years, traveled the same streets for 35 years and have lots of "contact" friends. And I keep looking for more.

I want to **know their story**. For some, it comes 5 minutes at a time, a month apart. For others, it may be a couple hours once a year. But I want to know and remember their story

Their story helps me **UNDERSTAND** them. To really understand them, we need to cross the racism bridge in many cases. Or to understand how adversity has made them who they are. People act and speak out of who they are; saying and doing what makes sense to them. To understand the output of their lives, we need to understand the input.

Then, the question is "what will we do with that understanding?" Lacking a better word, I am suggesting **LOYALTY** should result. And this loyalty is a two way street. You will need to trust them to be you friend as well as they need to trust that you will be yours. This loyalty might be a bit fragile. You may be hard for them to understand! But at some point, probably not a real distinct point, loyalty occurs. Or not.

So as they trust you, they may also trust Jesus in you.
You may be a part of a decision to activate their faith, perhaps using some of your faith, and commit to Christ. You may walk with them down the aisle at a church, you may pray with them in some setting or they may simply change in a way that you notice. Upon questioning, they may reveal a decision that made them different, even tho they don't know how to explain it.

As they begin to grow, they will become concerned more with others than themselves. They may want to see others grow in their relationship to Christ. In short, they begin to disciple others. Spiritual reproduction is a natural part of a life centered on Jesus.

They may move from being a spiritual parent to being a spiritual grandparent. That will change your role greatly, to being a peer rather than a mentor. This person will be about leading others and will need a different kind of assistance.

I want to generalize about group involvement.
Over time and years, most people participate and pass through a variety of group efforts. It could be church leadership, small group participation, hobby groups, study groups, etc. Within those groups, the previous individual levels of engagement may be occurring. In some cultures, individualism is frowned on, so people respond in groups. For each person, the Levels are a factor, but the response could be collective.

The MAJOR UNDERLYING PRESUPPOSITION is that we are always

working to help people attain another, deeper level.

Here is another representation of the concept of levels.

Want a "metric" to see how you are doing and what you might do next?

Then just do some counting and put a number down for what you are doing in each of the 8 levels.

A more printable copy of these Levels Of Engagement is at the end of this book. It is not Copyrighted and has room for names, so copy away!

As you count or list people in the various levels, what do you learn about your ministry with people?

LEVELS OF ENGAGEMENT for Intentional Relational Ministry

___1   **Acquaintance** in any setting, but particularly at home, work, or play —be *friendly*

___2   **Know** the outline of a person's **story** — **be a *good listener***

___3   Mutual **understanding** including cultural implications — mutual *trust*

___4   **Major commitment** to the other person's welfare— be *loyal*

___5   Offering **spiritual guidance**/discipleship, deciding to follow Jesus. Be *sharing/caring*

___6   Help them move from being self-centered to **others-centered— *making disciples***

___7   Coaching/training them to be a spiritual grandparent —*reproducing disciples*

___8   Doing people **planning t**o reach out as a group — *Jesus community/Church*

Here is a HUGE SECRET to Doing Ministry!—ASK QUESTIONS, THINK ABOUT THE ANSWERS!

Now to develop solid answers to the Levels, you need to be continually developing your skills at asking questions. Gentle questions, hard questions, soft questions, specific questions, general questions, leading questions, rhetorical questions, and any other kinds that are necessary! Where are your people really at?

This is crucial to helping people to learn and grow. Asking the questions.

You also must process the answers. Here are the questions for *you to answer:*

- *Where are they as a person, as a Follower of Jesus, and in their relationships to others?*

- *What is their next step in moving closer to Jesus, improving their relationships and caring for others?*

- *What is your part in that process?*

After people make a commitment to Jesus, we talk about becoming a Disciple. You can derive what is needed by simply answering these questions:

- *What should they KNOW?*

- *What should they BE?*

- *What should they DO?*

Now the trouble starts! We all bring our own notions of **Know-Be-Do**. Not surprisingly, we tend to do what was done with us. For many people it seems like **a Sunday School kind of thing**. Others, who may have met up with a real "following Jesus" effort in college, it seems like **conferences, Bible Study and weekly group meetings.** Still others, who may have come along later, **it is all about Church.** Most of the street-city folks will fall into the latter situation.

Consider the differences in some discipleship areas considering Intentionalists or Survivalists:

A friend of mine, Navigator Staff Mike Slone, suggests that discipleship involves CHANGE in "5 C's." Taking those concepts, Let's look at a possible contrast between the two worlds of Intentionalists and Survivalists:

1. *Commitments* – I need to note that Survivalists have some strong commitments. They tend to be made toward people and relationships rather than goals and stuff. **"You are with who you are with"** is a street expression for the commitment of individuals to a group when they move about. If I am walking with a group and have a strong commitment to them and they are attacked, so am I. Their "beef" is my beef. Merely walking with friends can be a life or death commitment on the street. I need to also note that relationships between Survivalists also tend to be more about a transaction than unconditional love. Typically, there is little enough love to go around, so it is rationed. But the transactional love is a strong force. Transactional love is a relationship based on mutual equal exchange. For example, the unemployed man stays with the welfare woman because she feeds/houses him and he protects her and the house from any kind of assault.

Commitments on the part of Intentionalists tend toward the propositional, commitments for Survivalists tend toward the personal. This also shows up in how the Bible is viewed. Survivalists have great appreciation for the characters, history in the Bible and the personhood of Jesus. I see Intentionalists ready to fall on their sword over systematic theology, the assertions of their interpretive community, and the preservation of their way of life. That is a real difference in what commitment means pragmatically.

2. *Character* – In the Intentionalist world, it tends to be defined by accomplishment more than intentions of the heart. It is about certain virtues; like *willpower, effort* and *success*. However, *acceptance, trust,* and *compassion* might be more of a Survivalist list. For the Survivalist, it means overlooking past travesty, even the horrible, and giving people another chance…over and over again. People with serious addiction problems often need many "rehab" efforts. What is important to the addict is the willingness of others to walk that road again…albeit with some rule changes!!

3. *Convictions* – What are the non-negotiables in a person's life? For the self-determined, the list is clear and often growing. Not so much for the Survivalist. He or she may have started down the road to Jesus from a very lawless place. I think there is a belief among Intentionalists that the strong Christian has a rather large list of rules to be believed and obeyed. In their view, perhaps, a disciple lives to add to that list and to practice obedience, because there is a belief that God supports the obedient and ignores the disobedient. Perhaps for the Survivalist it is more about relationships and a willingness to cross boundaries to support those relationships. The point where a self-centered Survivalist decides to focus on others for THEIR

benefit, takes commitment and conviction to care for someone else, possibly without getting anything back, is a milestone.

4. *Competency* – the Intentionalist strongly desires to be a journeyman disciple. Whatever a disciple of Jesus should ***Know , Be***, and ***Do***, Intentionalists want to be on that case. The difficulty comes when persons who are mostly failures in life seek to be disciples. Success is still very difficult. I think this is a hard one for most Christians to understand. Is Christianity mostly for "winners"? So what about the "losers"? What does the "Gospel for Losers" look like? If we look again at the 12 Apostles, how many of them were "losers" by their cultural standards? If we say that competency includes "loving one another," as expressed by Jesus in John 13:34, 35, "By this will all men know you are my disciples if you love one another," how do we quantify that? Can we perfect a "love dipstick" whereby the level of love in a person's heart can be plumbed? Is that more important than memorizing parts of the Bible? Perhaps we need standards of passion, compassion and acceptance for Survivalist "losers" as well for the Intentionalist "winners." Losers may not "win" by "winner" standards, but they can win by God's standards. Are we clear about what God is really saying to "losers"?

5. *Calling* – This likewise has a greater appeal to the Intentionalist. To the goal-centered person, a CALL is very important. But I think there is a simple point of turning for both the Intentionalist and the Survivalist. It is that move away from being self-centered to being others centered. The Apostle Paul in his letter to the Galatians says, **"You, my brothers, were called to be free, but do not use your freedom to indulge the sinful nature; rather, serve one another in love. The entire law is summed up in a single command: Love your neighbor as yourself."** When the addict becomes more concerned about the addiction of others, when the protection of the weak become the agenda of the strong and when it becomes more important to give than to receive, the real call to the follower of Jesus comes to the forefront.

Perhaps one of the secrets to discipling others is to not try to make them like you but to be sure you understand where THEY are and what they already Know-Be-Do. Then ask the questions of them and others, "What do you FEEL the need for? By the way, don't confuse this with neediness. This is the kind of need related to growth not a need to survive.

THEN start answering those three questions…Know…be…do. Write up an individual plan for the next steps you may want to take with the person…or persons.

You Are My Best Friend...

It began with a property purchase in the inner city. I started working on a three story, three-unit building in hopes of getting it ready to rent quickly. Alone one morning, I began by putting in a new aluminum window in the back of the first floor where one was totally missing. I have developed a technique for mixing mortar, literally by hand, in a 5 gal. bucket and using my hand to place it. Very sloppy in the best of times. In the middle of setting the metal window frame, a guy living next door came up to me , looked at my handful of mortar, and said, "Have you ever thought of using professional help?" I laughed out loud at both his choice of words and the impudence of them! "Are you a bricklayer?" I asked. He nodded. "Then go get your tools!" He set to work and I left the building in his hands, quite happy with how the day had gone.

The next morning as I arrived, I discovered the mortar had hardened in the bucket and the window was only half done. The non-rent paying sex worker who lived on the third floor told me, "Oh, they killed your bricklayer last night." That was not the way I liked starting my day!

Yes, Reggie had been shot 3 times by a 9mm handgun, but he survived… and about two months later, after he had recovered, he asked for his old job back. That began my relationship with him and three other young black men who lived nearby, some of them working for me off and on. All of them used heroin as frequently as they could afford it, so I ended up hiring and firing them multiple times over the next few years.

They came to me one day and asked if we could form a gang. They had a name, the" Duce Posse." I was never quite sure why they selected that name, but I accepted. We were a motley crew, but we all had our street names and had plans if we were challenged by a rival gang. Since I had a gun permit and was carrying all the time as a cash-accepting landlord, I was the cornerstone to our defense! Not that we needed one, my white skin was as good as a badge, even without the gun. It also helped that Reggie normally looked like he had just committed some major crime and could give pause to most people on the street with just a scowl. He once was surrounded by gun-wielding cops when he was trying to open a checking account in a local bank! However that could also have been the ski mask he was wearing.…….

It wasn't easy trying to get the gang together for any kind of organized meeting. It seemed like someone was always in jail or on the run. I remember an "intervention" type meeting where three of them were trying to get the fourth to stop getting high, even tho *they* were still getting high! We were meeting in a grubby basement, I was sitting on the world's nastiest sofa, while a pit bull puppy worked determinedly to chew my socks off.

"Country," was "on the box" which meant he had an ankle box that allowed him to be on home detention…and it was going off all the time. They turned to me and said, "Read a Psalm to us and pray." Which I did. All of them had made professions of faith and been baptized previously, but heroin and discipleship don't mix very well.

One day Reggie and I had done a small construction job somewhere and as we were arriving on his street, he turned to me and said, "You are my best friend!." That caught me by surprise…largely because he was not MY best friend! "Reggie, " I protested, "I am an old white man, you are a young black man, we are very different!."

"But you know my secrets, " he said. Gesturing to the street where he lived and the people in the street in front of it, "If they knew what you know about me, I would have to kill them!" I was happy to be his friend at that point, but made a mental note to be careful not to share his secrets!

It is some 20 years later now and Reggie has passed on to Glory. He got married several years after this incident, having found someone he could confide in, but was also a fan of heroin. He got the best of his addiction most of the time, but in the end, it got him. But not before he helped start a church and became a Deacon. It was a scraggly church, ultimately the pastor went back to cocaine and dropped out of the ministry and the church folded up, about the time Reggie passed on. It was also the sight of my most marathon Sunday service. We started at 11 am, I preached at about 1 and finally left about 6pm using some excuse. I heard it went until on till 9!

But that day of declared friendship still comes to mind even though it was long ago. "You're my best friend!" It still is a bit of a jolt to this day. You see, we live in a world, particularly the street world, where there is no one to trust with our secrets. Just the act of listening, without any thought of using those secrets against people, is an act of servanthood in the highest degree. I was rewarded one New Year's Eve, as I sat on the platform of my city church. I watched him come forward, collapse on the floor in front, sobbing like a baby, while he gave his life to Jesus…one more time. I carry Reggie's secrets to this day. He gave me a precious gift. His trust. If they can't trust you, how will they trust Jesus?

No, I am Not Going to Make More Suggestions! You Figure it Out!

I think it is always much easier to simply find a "pattern" and squeeze people into it. "Go to Seminary" is often the first suggestion many a young person receives upon declaring a desire to minister to people. Not surprisingly, the seminary suggested usually matches the cultural/spiritual/practical bent of the interpretive community around them. Little thought is given to what that seminary teaches along the lines of "Know-Be-Do." There is lots of "know," very little "be" and limited "do" …in many cases. Even with the better ones, there is a strong lack of reality.

Many seminaries require a doctrinal agreement before entry, during the time there and an agreement before leaving. While I did not complete seminary, I remember having hopes that what I did study would be useful. 40 years later, I cannot recall a single point that was useful ! I lost count of the number of pastors who have told me the same thing! I ended up in a very different place and with a much-revised theology. *(And I didn't have to sign an exit document)*

But I will offer another concept:
FILLING PRECEDES FRUITFULNESS

Think of yourself for a moment. Suppose a person or group, along with God, resolved to "pour" into your life, focusing on you, giving relational support, LIVED truth, enthusiasm, confidence and trust……So much that you could not help but **to pour the overflow out into another life.** Suppose that you and God put that overflow into another person, an EXCESS (not the minimum) of support, inspiration and God . **Don't you think that would result in that person having an overflow as well?**

I might boldly suggest that the lavish "pouring" in response to a person's desire to grow and know God, might result in significant growth of an entire church. Why? Because I have just described three generations of growing people. So if you joined the efforts **of relational support** of people in a city church, don't you think that would make a difference?

It's up to you. It is your life.

But to "pour" in confidence, you will need to appreciate how others have poured into you.. Just as we have discovered some "secrets" together, you should expect that you will find a God that you didn't know…when you look for His secrets in the City. So expect a BLESSING! And rewarding relationship with God… if that is what you really want.

Wrapping things up, here is what I have tried to do with this book:

1) Demonstrate that the subject of a city ministry is a large one that requires study, effort and personal change over time. Yet there is a micro side to it requiring understanding and personal contact.

2) Offer some additional ways to view some of the dimensions of city ministry because there are some real problems with what is currently being done by white-controlled efforts.

3) To suggest that the keys to real urban ministry are held **by adaptable white folks and the black (or other ethnicity) churches *who are already there.***

4) Establish some reference points so others need not make the same mistakes.

5) Throw in some practical tips.

6) Call out Racism.

7) Give hope to Millennials

8) Look at the core of ministry.

Now it is up to you. Just remember that if you are of a pale skin, your culture will suggest that you can get away with doing nothing. Remember White Privilege? If you are a "minority" but grew up in the suburbs, you might deny the need to connect back into the city. But you will most certainly miss out on part of what God is doing.

What I desperately hope is that you will find God in the City and be blessed by God's People.

Chapter 12

Stories & Thoughts

Folsom Prison Blues

"I see that train a-comin', its rollin' round the bend, but I ain't seen the sunshine, since I don't know when..." I mean, what other song makes sense to sing to a group of inmates, mostly 'ol country boys who got tired of being in the Army and went home? To their surprise, the FBI rolled into their town, locked them up for being AWOL, and shipped them to the closest Army stockade, where they cooled their heels until they out-processed. Not exactly hardened criminals, but then I was not a professional singer!

It started when my roommate, who was working at the Post Stockade (prison) thought we should do a "Campus Crusade" meeting for the inmates, since he had been well trained by them in college. Thanks to a bit of fast talking on my part, he was persuaded to join me in starting a Navigator ministry at the Post, but he wanted to do what was familiar. It worked on Campus in Oklahoma, so he thought it would work in a Tennessee prison. So we tried it.

The format was simple, put out the word that there would be a "Navigators Service" in the Chapel and anyone who wanted to attend should stand by their cell door to be allowed to attend. About half of the prison population would do just that, mostly out of boredom, so sometimes 100 men would be in the audience. I have always thought there was less of a difference between "Christian" music and "Secular" music that some claimed. Oh, the words were different but either seemed to hit the same spot in the soul. So, we usually "warmed up" with some lighter, popular songs, then a hymn and a couple testimonies. One of us would do a "Bridge Illustration" Gospel presentation and call for a response. It was not uncommon for 25-30 men to stand, indicating they wanted to be committed to Christ. We handed out "comment cards" which we used to follow up those who responded.

So I played my $15 guitar and sang "Folsom Prison Blues," with some major apologies to Johnny Cash. One of the comment cards indicated that I had wasted my money on singing lessons, but for the most part it was received well. I could stay on pitch and belt out the song, but with a voice as smooth as crushed rock.

Like any good Navigator, I focused on following up on those cards, by training my roommate and others to talk to the inmates. We had about 4 men who had various jobs in the Stockade and they were free to talk with the men who responded with a desire to grow in Christ. Those men recruited others who were not in the Stockade and the ministry at Fort Campbell began in 1971. It continues to this day, since the Post is the home of the 101st Airborne Division (Air Mobile) .

Now I don't think the ministry began because I sang "Folsom Prison Blues." But because Bob and I were willing to take a chance in starting a service, others were motivated to reach out. We grew from the two of us to more than 40 of us in a year or so. It was not the main thing we did, but it was a great way to help our disciples to share their testimony by standing up and delivering it to a captive audience!

My dream today still has men who were incarcerated as a part of it. Many of the men we need to come back and minister to our urban communities are currently "doing time." Many are in "churches" behind the walls, in Bible Studies and being discipled......... while incarcerated. We seek to connect them to local churches when they get out, to care for each other and to serve the communities they previously took from. There is room for lots of help from those who are outside, just like there was a need for them at the Fort Campbell Stockade.

"There's probably rich folks eatin', in a fancy dining car, they're probably drinking coffee and smoking big cigars.. But that train keeps a rollin', and that's what tortures me…" Not unlike campus or military ministry, there is a continuous inflow and outflow of people in our prison system. And it is relentless. The question is whether we will see the potential of the situation or be on the train headed in the other direction.

ALL DRIED UP

He was not a nice person by most standards; Steve did not "suffer fools gladly." An intelligent man, his disease and finances caused him to live in Section 8 housing, surrounded by lesser lights who spent their time foolishly…at least by his reckoning. And then there was his loss of dignity because of the chronic diarrhea he suffered, caused by an active case of Acquired Immune Deficiency Syndrome, (AIDS). He retaliated by simply living nude! Any ruckus that involved his building or his apartment he simply dealt with ….without clothes. He was not a pleasant sight, since being bedridden over time does not improve one's physique. Of course the Police were called, but they wanted nothing to do with a man visited by AIDS, who was caustic and articulate. Some officers needed convincing, so he would invite them into his apartment and point out the array of drugs and needles he needed to stay alive and that would need to be transported with him if arrested. They would simply order him to stay in his apartment (like he could leave) and drive off quickly!

This behavior was a constant thorn to the neighbors, who seemed to thrive on drama. It is difficult for the sub-urban dweller to grasp low-income, high-density life. Life in the low-income city is simply relationally intensive, fueled by loud communication, distorted information and abject accusations….which must all be verbally sorted out without regard to the time of day. They, of course, were oblivious to the many ways they irritated Steve, including the one he hated most, PITY.

He claimed that he got HIV from a bad transfusion, however his choice of magazines for the bathroom indicated a focus on men rather than women. Be that as it may, he was cared for by the Gay community in a way that would make Jesus proud. From food to cleaning the apartment to transportation to doctor visits, Steve was well loved. But he hated pity. As the Manager of the building for a non-profit, I got involved with his apartment maintenance and, of course, the constant battle between the other residents who felt sorry for him but hated him as well.

To get his respect, I had to show neither pity nor weakness. Further, I had to debate his assertions on a pseudo-intellectual level. It usually started with my ringing his doorbell and yelling, "Are you dead yet?" then opening his apartment door and walking in a couple seconds later. He didn't lock his door because he couldn't always get up to open it. So a part of his torture was 24 hour vulnerability…which is why he needed the neighbors to keep an eye on him, but not get too involved in his life. A tenuous prospect. I knew this so I simply walked in after my courtesy doorbell and started in on him. "Not dead yet, I see…" Which made him smile! We then proceeded to talk in a language and manner not taught in Church. I have long made it a habit to learn the language spoken by the people and to be comfortable with the words used by them to communicate. No, it really only means learning a handful or two of words that one uses like salt and pepper…and seasons to taste. But the inflections are everything…

"So where are you going to go when you die?" was my subtle way to talk about spiritual things. He was skilled at deflecting, since he thought himself a religious expert. However, in an indirect way, he shared bits and pieces of where he was at. He had at T-cell count of 7, so he named them Matthew, Mark, Luke and John.......and Larry, Curly and Moe!

"Jesus was the Son of God," he would say, "and so was Mohammad, Buddha and the Dali Lama." With some banter and poking, I found out that he was particularly sad because a girl that he loved had gotten HIV from him and had already died *(which altered my perceptions of some people's sexuality)*. Each time he disclosed something major about his life, thoughts or feelings, he was quick to deflect it and to water it down. "But maybe it was some other guy" he said. "Nope," I said, "you are just too great a lover for that to happen," using my own deflection.

I would stop in to see him whenever I felt like it. It was a particularly down time of life for me, with many struggles. At that time I did not see myself as much of a missioner. I was trying to resemble Jesus, but it was not easy being a Landlord. Later, Steve did give me a beautiful wreath he had made out of dried flowers when he was stronger. He had a business making the wreaths...he called the business, "All Dried Up"! He began fading more rapidly and his T-cells went to none.

One day I stopped by using my usual greeting, but this time it was different. I could sense it when I walked into the room. "What happened to you?" I asked. "Did Jesus come for you?" He smiled in a radiant sort of way and said, "Yes, and he brought Paul and Moses." I didn't get a chance to talk more, we were interrupted by something, probably a commotion in the hallway. And he died not long after.

I suppose I talked to him for 10-30 minutes on perhaps 8 occasions. Most of it banter and blather. But I think I communicated compassion rather than pity and encouragement rather than judgment. He knew I was different, that I appreciated him and didn't take myself too seriously. But the blessing was all mine. I had a chance to see what God saw and most other people didn't. And I got to see what God does ...without much help from me. I remember Steve whenever we put up that wreath. "All Dried Up." What a joy to realize he is not his business name anymore! No dried-up wreaths in Heaven!

FIRE IN THE CITY

The sight of the black smoke from a house fire is unmistakable in the city. High density housing, in the form of row houses, is simply a tinderbox. It doesn't take much to get a blaze going and even the smallest fire effects the houses on either side. For the poor, a fire is both a frequent occurrence and a devastating one.

Now I am no hero, but I have run into a building that was on fire on more than one occasion. It is really no big deal, not like on TV. Once it was a man smoking in bed. I and another construction worker broke down the screen door and rushed upstairs. The blaze had started with the mattress from the resident smoking in bed. The man was almost unconscious, so we carried him out … in his underwear! As he came to, he realized that fact and that he was the object of some stares from the neighborhood women, so he ran back into the house! We carried the smoldering mattress outside while he found his pants. Not much damage, tho if the smoke had not been noticed, the man might not have survived. The fire department finally arrived and made a show of tearing up the man's mattress and drowning it with water.

One spring day I was driving in my city and saw the smoke. I jumped out and ran to the house, only to be met with frantic parents who were carrying out two small children, perhaps 2 and 3. Now, I am not fond of kids (other than my own and the grandchildren) but I took the two of them and their shoes. I carried them a couple houses away and sat with them on the neighbor's marble steps. As I put their shoes on, I talked to them.

"Oh, look, here comes the fire truck! See the men are hooking the hose to a hydrant? Your mom and dad are getting some of your stuff out of the house for you," and whatever else I could think of to say. There I was, a strange man, holding the two children closely while I talked to them in a low voice. I helped each of them with their shoes, putting them on and lacing them up. I could feel them tremble from time to time, but I talked and helped them observe. We sat together for perhaps 15 minutes, tho it felt like hours.

A women came up then and said with conviction that she was their mother's sister. The kids seemed to recognize her and she took them to a waiting car a little distance from the fire. The smoke had shifted from black to white, signaling that the fire was being put out. Since I could think of nothing else to do, I simply got into my car and left.

But I left with a warm, amused feeling. Is anything greater than to jump into an emergency, do something that is significant for another person, who will never know your name? And then to melt away before the backslapping begins? A significant deed done, only a few minutes sacrificed and a positive outcome. No TV/Cable News to contend with, no fawning admirers and no excessive thank-yous. Just a moment in time that God and I could enjoy. And some time praying for the parents, their kids and their future.

Peanut Breath

We had an office just half a block from the Junction. It was a hotspot for all sorts of activities in my large Eastern city, which tended to produce "characters." Or perhaps the characters produced the activities. Sometimes the characters came inside our office abruptly, like the time 6-8 male teens grabbed the Gum Ball Machine, placed in the office to raise money for the Lions Club. Since things in the City have a way of getting distorted, it was filled with Peanut M &M's!

They appeared to be on their way home from school and were minor characters in the street theatre of the Junction, so no one noticed them…until they flung open the office door, grabbed the M & M machine and departed in haste. The receptionist let out a yell and a couple of us ran to the rear of the building, chuckling, jumped into our radio-equipped plumbing vans and gave chase. Not much of a chase, since they had disappeared. However, the receptionist was also the radio operator and she had called the police. A couple police cars joined the pursuit, which added to the drama.

We passed some rundown garages with their doors ajar and stopped to check inside. A cop and I discovered the broken machine, money missing and most of the peanut M &M's as well. He relayed the discovery to his associates and just as quickly a band of protesting juveniles were grabbed by them several blocks away. Dashing to our respective vehicles, the cop in his car and I in my van, we were soon on the scene. There was much protesting on the part of the Juveniles. Denials abounded. However, many of them seem to have an excess of quarters in their pockets…tho hardly a cause for arrest.

The female officer who had stopped them had them lined up like a Drill Sargent inspecting the troops. It was an amusing sight, 5 or 6 cop cars and a couple plumbing trucks surrounding a gaggle of uncomfortable minority teens. Suddenly there was a breakthrough in the case!

"Breathe on me again!," said the cop to a teen she was questioning. He complied, though somewhat puzzled. "You got peanut M & M's on your breath!" , she yelled in triumph! She was quickly joined by a couple other officers who went down the line of teens smelling each one's breath. About 5 were soon selected and charged with the crime! I suspect it was a break-through in law enforcement, the determination of guilt by peanut breath!

Of course this was all met with a great deal of laughter, jeers and catcalls from the officers and the bystanders. As the Wagon arrived to pack up the youthful thieves, we went back to the office chuckling at how Justice could be amusing in goofy ways. I could just see the teens in school the next day.

"Man, we got locked up for NOTHIN'! That *(female dog)* locked us up because we had M &M's on our breath!" Wonder if they will tell that story to their grandchildren!

So what does your breath smell like? Something that can get you locked up? Or perhaps just rejected? We all hope that we smell like Jesus, at least in some way. It is not a crime to eat peanut M & M's, even in Christian circles, tho perhaps your Weight Watchers meeting might feel differently. At any rate, what we chew on is important…as well as where it come from!!

WHEN THE ENGINE QUITS

I was upside down when the engine quit. Gas was dumping on the wind-shield and since it was an open-cockpit airplane, it was hitting the top of my head. Self-taught aerobatics didn't seem like such a good idea after all…

It all began a couple years earlier when I bid on an airplane engine on eBay, which came with a disassembled small biplane. It was built by a dentist in his spare time, some years previous. I was the high bidder, so I paid and picked it up. Since the plane seemed in such good condition, I put it back together, over a couple years' time with some modifications, got the engine running, got it inspected and began to fly it. However, the problem with a single-seat airplane is that there is no place for a flight instructor. I had to learn things for myself.

If you learn by trial and error, you should expect errors, perhaps more than your share. The wise aviator spends much of their practice time preparing for the errors, usually pilot errors. To fly multi-engine planes, for example, much of the time is spent preparing to fly on just one engine! Of course, there are books, seminars, and flight instructors to cover the basics. There are rules upon rules, Federal inspectors, flight tests and check rides, to insure as much as possible that people are qualified to fly and that the airplanes are more likely to fly than fail.

But once you are alone in the plane, chose to shove that throttle forward and achieve flying speed, books, seminars, rules, advice, videos and pep talks evaporate from your mind! As the wheels leave the ground, it is just you, your airplane and, of course, God. Once your wings are carrying the weight, you leave the hangar behind.

I have always thought there were a lot of parallels between "committing aviation" and "walking with God." Books on Flying and of course the Bible have a lot in common. Both discuss how NOT to do it as well as how TO do it. But neither offers enough to fully teach the art of either flying or walking with God. Now some of you who read this have likely overreacted at that statement. But think about it, if you try to fly by only reading a book, you will almost certainly die. If you read the Bible and ignore the guidance of the Holy Spirit and experienced Christians, you are likely to crash and burn over something as well. The problem is not the writings of the Book, but rather the interpretation. Lived truth comes from the mix of truth and experience.

"To do an aileron roll, enter at cruising speed, pitch up 20 degrees, center the controls and quickly move the control stick to its full left or right travel and hold it against the stop." Simple, right? As it turns out, doing rolls is one of those things that can be screwed up easily. And after several successful attempts, I used a bit too much forward stick, which resulted in a slightly negative "g" load when I should have kept it positive. That dumped fuel out the cap but more importantly, it kept fuel in the carburetor instead of letting it go into the engine. So it quit.

We all find "former Christians" who lacked a learning relationship with an older Christian, so they made a move that starved their spiritual engine. And it quit. Or rather they did. God and gravity don't really change much. We are the variables. And it doesn't take much for us to lose faith.

When I lost power, the nose pitched down, I rolled the airplane right side up and waited for an eternity, while looking for a place to land. I suppose it was only 4 seconds before the engine roared back to life, once the carburetor could do its job. But it seemed much longer. For the Christian who fails in some way, it can likewise seem like an eternity before contact is established with God again. I went back to the airstrip and landed, taking a break for a while. When I was ready and had carefully understood what I did wrong,

I took off and did more rolls. And I tell my story. "Don't go negative in the middle of a roll!" is my admonition for pilots.

In the spiritual world, being upside-down and powerless may also happen. So, first get right side up again. Then the power will come back. Make adjustments, usually in your attitude, and fly on. We need you.

A MISUSE OF POWER?

I was in Iowa recently talking with a retired gentleman who I had known for my whole life. He had visited me in Baltimore briefly some years ago and wanted to share a story that involved a black person in Iowa. I think he told me the story because while he affirmed the events, he was uncomfortable somehow with the conclusion.

He worked in a small manufacturing business and observed that the owner/boss hired a young black man. The new man was put to work with my friend doing a menial task. That involved working with a partner to move a stack of large pipe. That task was completed but the next one had not begun. So, the young man sat down. Shortle, the owner appeared. He had a reputation for not liking to see men sitting or standing around during work time. He asked the young man why he was sitting down.

"I'm tired." Said the man. "Yes," said the owner, "but I am paying you to work, not sit down, so I need you to get busy."

The young man complied …until the Boss was out of sight. And he sat down again to rest. However, the boss was just around the corner and he suspected the young man might sit down again. He looked around the corner, observed the sitting down and moved to confront the young man.

"Why are you sitting down?" the young man was asked. "I'm tired" was the reply. "Follow me, " said the boss, and the two of them walked into his office.

Taking a checkbook, the boss wrote out a check. "Here is your pay for today, I cannot use you any further," he said, handing the young man the check. "I must have people who will accomplish work and not sit down"

For most people who have worked in a labor-intensive environment in Iowa, this story would ring true. If pressed, they would admit that they know the start of a new job has its humilities, pain and struggle. Few of us are prepared for a labor-intensive effort. However, we have faith that it will get better and that we will be able to physically adjust to the effort in time. And we understand a boss who does not want people standing around.

I live across the street from a black man who is a retired General Motors worker. He describes the difficulty of keeping up with a fast-moving vehicle assembly line. He also describes how hard it was at the start and on other occasions. He had both black and white supervisors, but it was all about keeping the assembly line moving. But he also came from a farm background and understood what was expected when you went to work. And then there is Mike, an older black man who is devoted to my son's business. Mike is the first one there in the morning, the last one to leave at night… almost 7 days a week. He is nearly indispensable. Always on his feet. Always moving. Race, at least anecdotally, is not the obvious problem. So what was? After all, a man needed a job. Now he still does.

We all have expectations. We all are products of our culture. We all struggle with understanding each other when there are cultural differences. And then there are adaptations.

What if this had happened? What if the boss made this speech to the young man?

"We work hard here. We must to survive. One of my expectations is that no one sits around. Every person who works here is important. Even the smallest effort has an impact. But at the beginning, the job you will have will be tiring. I need you to work through that. If you need to sit down, go to the bathroom and sit on the toilet (I actually did this when I worked at a factory one summer). But don't sit in the workplace unless your job requires it. You must be an example to everyone and everyone must be an example to you. I want you to become a long -term employee like many of the others. I want to promote you as fast as I can, but you will have to earn it."

"I will be watching you… to appreciate your efforts and to correct them. I want you to do well."

Some employees need a lot of affirmation when they start. Some need careful correction. But if the highest value of African-Americans is **Dignity and Respect**, they will not do well in settings where this does not occur. If the highest value of Caucasians, particularly Europeans, is getting things done, they will not be happy without working at a fast pace. So, there can be a conflict of expectations. And the boss wins, because he has the power. Or does he win? Losing good employees is a recipe for a struggling business.

Who wouldn't like an employee like Mike? Or my neighbor? I cant help wondering, if the owner had a bit more cultural understanding, that an opportunity was missed. White privilege means owners DON'T have to understand culture, they can usually find someone who will understand the Owners Culture. But young men who lacked a familiarity with the owners expectations, but have potential, have a hard time getting started. This is what my city friends faced. Out of shape, they had problems doing manual labor. Mentally unprepared, they found it difficult to follow orders. Having little ego strength, they were sensitive to the smallest slight. Which made them difficult to employ.

If there is a single factor in changing lives, it is employment. A job can lead to marriage rather then just being a "baby daddy," it can lead to self-confidence, it can lead to being a taxpayer, it can lead to support of a church, it can mean a break in multi- generational poverty…to name a few. In short, it is the difference between night and day.

So, help people get and keep jobs…

CHASING A TOILET

I got a bargain on some toilets, so I put a new one in an apartment I was trying to rent. Not that it would be a key rental attraction, but more of an attempt to lower my maintenance costs in the future. Then I got a call from another tenant in the building, who excitedly said, "they are stealing your TOILET!" I told them to hang up and call the police, I was on my way.

I arrived shortly after the Police and I guess it was a slow morning for them in Baltimore. There was already a description of the getaway vehicle, which was quickly discovered by the Police Helicopter and a hot pursuit was underway! The reporting resident explained a guy had broken into the vacant apartment, pulled out the toilet and had sold it to the fleeing thief.

"They got him surrounded on Baltimore Street, get in your van and follow me" Said the excited Cop on the scene. He went lights and siren, so I got on his tail and we went tearing to the traffic stop.

Five minutes later I was walking past about 8 police cars and a circling helicopter to identify the stolen toilet in the back of a beat-up station wagon. The handcuffed driver was protesting vigorously that he had simply bought the toilet, which cost me $75, for $20. When he saw me, he switched from protesting into begging. "Please, Mister, I just needed a new toilet! It was only $20"! Please don't let them lock me up"! I was unmoved.

I made the identification requested, the police transport van arrived, as did the tow truck which hauled his station wagon to the impound yard. But not before I retrieved the evidence, a nice, new toilet, slightly smudged. There was no effort to retain the evidence before the trial, since the man admitted to "buying" the toilet in front of the address of my building.

About 4 months later, I received the subpoena requiring my presence at the "toilet trial" as a key witness for the prosecution. At the court, I was again lobbied by the Defendant to "drop the charges." He proclaimed that he was sorry, that it cost him over $500 for bail, tow fees and a consultation with an attorney…who was not present. I told him I was sorry, but that I would let the Court decide.

I had a lot of experience in Baltimore Courts and what happened was what I suspected. He was given a Nolle Prosequi, or a Nolle Pross. Which simply means, "We ain't gonna do nothing with this." Judges do have good sense. All this fuss over a toilet, which had cost a man a day in jail and significant money. It was a legitimate arrest but the crime was not that significant. And I believe justice was served. I doubt that man will be looking for cheap toilets anytime soon. Particularly stolen ones.

The hard-living part of the city is full of this type of crime. Small thefts are typically not pursued with the same reckless abandon as my toilet. Most of the time, the thief simply escapes…to steal again, and again. Much of the crime in Baltimore is simply opportunistic. An opportunity presents itself for the transfer of property, services or favor from one person to another… over the objections of the transferee. Courts rarely give much more than a slap on the hand for such theft. Police rarely follow up on the many theft reports that they write up. So, people who live in the tough areas become opportunistic themselves. No, the man didn't remove the toilet from my property, but he was a willing recipient and did pay the $20 to someone who was never caught.

This means that people who work in the city, be they clergy, resident or service tech, become numb to the loss of property, the availability of stolen goods and the lack of prosecution. It is no surprise, then, that thieves move from property to simple mugging…the taking of the wallet or purse at gun-point. They overlook that such is a felony, "armed robbery" and will involve a significant time in prison…as exemplified by O. J. Simpson.

Those who interact with hard-living urban dwellers have ethics issues to consider. How do we deal with crime …and the criminal?

This story is humorous because it has a clownish factor to it. It is silly at its core. But not so silly to the thief that gets caught.

THANK YOU, BUSTER

He was an old black man who had few friends and fewer still who understood him. His story could have been the story of many other black men in Baltimore, except that Buster could have been more.

He was a bright young man in the 1940s who could have gone to college and done well. But something happened, which he refused to talk about. Instead, he lived the life of a dockworker, a Baltimore Longshoreman. In those days, cargo like bananas was unloaded by hand. He was simply one of a thousand who supplied the labor on an intermittent basis for a number of years. There were good times and bad times, but he relied on his back not his brain for his income. But then mechanization and age made his work difficult to find.

I met him in the 1980's when he was an old day laborer who mostly dug holes and shoveled dirt. Every weekday morning, he would arrive very early at Dennison Plumbing (he was so trusted he had a key to the door) and read his newspaper until he was given a work assignment. Some days he just carried tools and materials, some days he used a shovel. Other days he got $30 for just showing up and was sent home.

On several occasions, he went with me as I accepted underground piping jobs to make ends meet. He was slow. And......methodical. In my ignorance and youth, sometimes I tried to get him to move faster. He responded by maintaining the same pace, but grinding his teeth! He would say nothing, but his false teeth made quite a racket as he ground them with ever increasing speeds! He never complained, but we knew he was not happy!

When I complained about him, my friend Jay looked at me in disbelief and said, "He is an old man who makes $50 or $75 a day in cash. What do you expect?" Chagrined, I changed my attitude.

At the time Susan Butcher was perhaps America's Greatest Athlete as she won the Iditarod multiple times. As I walked into the office one morning, I asked the group standing around, "How is Susan Butcher doing in the Iditarod," not expecting anyone to know or care.

"At 5 o'clock this morning, she was running first," Said Buster.

I was stunned. Had I missed something about Buster? Could he be much more than he seemed?

As time went on, I had more short conversations with him. He was a bright man who chose his words in a deliberate understatement. One day we dropped him off to hand-dig a water service. When we went back to check on him a couple hours later, he had accomplished little with his proverbial pick and shovel. He greeted us with:

"I'm wondering what sins I have committed that made me have to dig this hole. Do you think God is mad at me?" he said with his eyes twinkling.

The ground was indeed just like concrete. It was as bad as trying to dig through rock. We rented a backhoe to do the job.

A couple years later, Buster's health had deteriorated and he was unable to work or do much. He didn't lose his sense of humor. "The Doctor said I have a weakness. My left side is weak. I guess he thought I didn't notice…"

As he failed in health, we moved him to an apartment of ours and we didn't bother to collect rent. I remembered the sadness of two things. One was that he handled depression by simply getting a bottle of whiskey with his Friday pay and locking himself in his apartment for the weekend. Monday was a new beginning.

The second was a past common-law marriage that ended after 20 years with his wife's death. Her relatives came up from North Carolina and simply cleaned out his house. They loaded their car with as much as they could and tied the furniture on top with ropes, while Buster stood quietly by. "They didn't even leave me a chair to sit on," he recalled. I can only imagine the grief and pain of his loss, of wife, furniture and no one to share his grief.

Buster was not a fighter. Somewhere in his youth, despite the urging of his mother, he simply gave up hope. In short, probably due to racism, he treated his own hurts and pain by simply swallowing them. He was a wry observer of the human condition, but refused to risk his life for it…… thereby losing it anyway.

There was something about Buster that indicated he might have been a significant person. He was a thinker and an observer. But Baltimore City in the old days was not particularly nurturing of black boys with potential… but lacking a certain amount of will to overcome the obstacles of race, class and poverty.

I can do little now but simply remember Buster. But I hope you will join me in looking for other Busters in the making, giving them some encouragement, hearing their story, sitting with them in life and calling them to rise above their circumstances. Be Jesus to them.

Thank you, Buster. You meant more to me than I ever said in life. I'm sorry I didn't know you better.

BROWNIE DIES

As I was transitioning out of campus ministry and into being a landlord, I acquired Brownie. I learned a lesson the day he died. Oh, he wasn't a person but rather a beat-up Chevy Van. I had turned it into a rolling hardware store, filled with plumbing fittings in metal-drawered cabinets along with a large inventory of property maintenance materials and tools. A lot of stuff.

At the time, I was acting a bit like a vigilante, so I had borrowed a portable police scanner. I was on my way to a meeting, running late and driving too fast when I got distracted by a police call which was on my way. Which meant I missed the stop sign and got in front of a speeding taxi. It was a classic T-Bone crash with me as the top cross bar. It was just before the serious seat belt enforcement started and I was not wearing one. I suddenly found myself sitting on top of the engine "dog house" as we flew across the intersection and slammed into the side of a brick rowhouse. I remember thinking, "Oh, this is going to be expensive!"

It was a little difficult to crawl out the window and I was shaken up a bit. Since it was a warm day, the crash brought all the neighbors out to look and watch. The people in the Taxi were not seriously hurt, and since they were being attended to , I just waited by Brownie.

So there I was, the only white-skinned person among a couple hundred and the obvious cause of the crash. I had not seen the stop sign because the view from Brownie was blocked by series of "No Parking" signs which were at exactly the right height to obstruct my view. But to the people around me, it was obvious I was the cause of the crash and the cause of the injured people. As I stood quietly, the woman whose house I hit offered to let me use her phone, which I did. When I came out the Police were there, but they were occupied by a disturbance over the people in the Taxi. I heard one of the officers say, "If you don't shut up, I will lock you up!"

A bit later, my tow truck showed up and I gave my information to the Police. They were black also, but were kind and cordial. They did not give me a ticket for missing the Stop sign.

No one said the slightest negative word to me. They seemed to understand that I screwed up but didn't think it was their responsibility to chastise me for it. There was no animosity toward me, only kindness. Now, if I had decided to be belligerent for some reason, or shoot off my mouth, that might have been a great deal different. But I wasn't, it was my fault that I missed the stop sign.

The death of Brownie was helpful when some years later I walked among the crowd during the aftermath of the Freddie Gray Uprising. I knew the good heartedness of Baltimore. I knew they didn't blame all white people, just the Police who misbehaved on a regular basis. Besides, on the second day things had simply turned into a Baltimore Block Party!

UNRECOGNIZED

I love Atlanta. For a lot of reasons. But the one that pops into my head now involves Reverend Dr. Martin Luther King, Jr… Because I owe him an apology. I always will.

Years ago, as a Navigator college student in southern Minnesota, I was sitting in my dorm room one day when I heard on the radio that he had been shot and killed. I uttered these horrible words, *out loud*, even though I was alone…

> *Well, now that he is gone, maybe those Negroes will calm down.*

What an idiot I was!

The next semester, my roommate took an African-American studies class, and I started reading his books. *Black Like Me, Autobiography of Malcom X,* and *Black Boy*. Horror slowly crept over my soul as I began to realize the truth of the "African American experience," to use the ultimate understatement. With growing momentum, over the years, I realized I owed a debt for my words and my ignorance.

So, I try to visit his grave every time I am in Atlanta. One time early on, I was given an insider's after-hours tour by a King family member with a group of InterVarsity staff.

My routine is spending a few personal moments in a particular spot. Through tears and sobs, I say,

> *"I'm sorry, I'm sorry, for what I said! I didn't know. I didn't know."*

So far, it hasn't helped much. Sometimes it seems like there is *too much to be forgiven* and it will take multiple visits. Oh, I know what the Bible says about grace, but the hurt runs deep.

On my second visit, I was with a group of Navigators some years back as we were trying to put together the "Nav Urban Network," the first of the attempts to link people who were working in the inner city. We had a great time, but it was soon over and I found myself walking through Hartsfield-Jackson International Airport on the way home. I noticed something curious.

An older black woman of conservative dress was making her way along the large carpeted corridor, accompanied by a couple younger women. I noticed that all the white people walked past her as though she wasn't there… or at least as if she wasn't significant. As most black people passed her, they stopped in their tracks, put their hand over their mouth in surprise, or whirled and stared at her back. As she passed, I turned and followed her for some distance just to take in the experience. For the length of the corridor, she was recognized by some and ignored by many.

I knew who she was, because I had just seen her picture on the wall at the grave. Yes, it was Coretta Scott King! She is no longer with us, but I wonder if that same experience was repeated for most of her life. She meant nothing to nearly all white people, yet was highly respected by African Americans. Ironically, what is known as "Martin Luther King Day" had recently been celebrated when I saw her, but obviously white folks had made little connection to her.

So I continue to say "I'm sorry!" to her husband, and I continue to take a lesson from her. Often the people you help the most are the least aware of it. White folks think that MLK's major contribution was to the lives of black people. But was it? Without him, wouldn't a whole lot of white folks have been trapped by their own ignorance? Some of us believe his major contribution was, in fact, the freeing of white folks from **their sins of racism**, and the slow death of a particular non-gentleman called Jim Crow. King helped **free whites of their foolishness in believing they were a superior race**, and thus authorized to treat people of color unjustly and deny them basic human rights.

As I head back to Atlanta in a few days, I will be just another overweight old white man walking along the carpets and getting on the train to the main terminal. I wasn't noticed before, and I won't be noticed now. Yet, there is a lesson from Coretta Scott King.

Some may notice us and most may not, but there are always people to love, business to attend to, and places to go. Noticed or not, we are on a journey. Hopefully out of ignorant racism.

Thank You

The following black folk have influenced me greatly and I owe them profoundly:

Dr. Elward Ellis, now in Glory, Pastor and former Director of Black Campus Ministry for InterVarsity. Along with his wife, Dawn Swaby-Ellis, M.D.

Dr. Bob Price, Professor and former long-term Navigator staff

Rev. Stan Long, Pastor, former InterVarsity Staff in the Baltimore Area

Bishop James Adams, Pastor of Dynamic Deliverance Cathedral, my "Cover "and Friend.

Dr. Carl Ellis, Professor, Teacher, friend and source of the "Intentionalist, survivalist" concepts

NavStaff Eugene Burrell and his wife, Diane. Their wedding was the first black church service I ever attended, 42 years ago. He is a "Soldier in the Army of the Lord" and has been more patent with me than anyone ever. His highest compliment is, "Kayberg, you are Crazy!"

NavStaff Marvin Campbell and his wife Pamela. He has been my strongest encouragement to be a part of the Navigators again. His friendship and humility is the greatest.

Bishop Kenneth Savage, Founder of Holy Truth Tabernacle, Street Preacher and mentor.

Rev. Dr. Phyllis Felton, the former leader of the Presbyterian, "Harambee Project" in Baltimore, Pastor of Madison Avenue Presbyterian Church

And, **Seymore Williams, MD; Dr. Brad Braxton, Dr. Stephanie Boddie, Ralph Brown and Reggie Toney.** I regret that I need to stop at this point, I would otherwise have hundreds to thank. I stand on the shoulders of humble giants.

whose actions are often difficult to predict as he is always up to something! Fortunately, they are grown, married, and living in their own homes…and made Doug a grandfather of six.

In the church world, Doug is a Presbyterian Elder in the Presbyterian Church USA as well as an Ordained Apostolic Pentecostal Pastor. "It works if you don't ask too many questions", he says. "But in reality, it is about relationships". His devotion to learning the city, doing the work God has lead him to do for over 30 years, has paid off and is illustrated in the contents of this book.

His desire to bring about true fellowship between black and white churches is a driving force in his ministry efforts. He is encouraging white congregations to take the lead by reaching out to include others with cultural differences. This could have the potential to change Sunday services across America…transforming the present day environment from "exclusive to inclusive", and from "segregated to integrated" and all the while, bringing glory to God.

Doug has lived his life serving others since 1965, when as a college freshman, he resolved to spend his life submitted to serve God in ways that benefit others. He seeks to apply the Scripture that says,

"Therefore my beloved brothers, be ye steadfast, immovable, always abounding in the work of the Lord, for you know that your labor is not in vain in the Lord."

I Corinthians 15:58

LEVELS OF ENGAGEMENT
FOR INTENTIONAL RELATIONAL MINISTRY

To evaluate where you are, list the numbers of people you know for each catagory, or list their names under the desription.

_____1) **Acquaintance** in any setting, but particularly at home, work or play — be *friendly*

_____

_____

_____2) **Know** the outline of a person's **story** — **be a** *good listener*

_____

_____

_____3) Mutual **understanding** including cultural implications — mutual *trust*

_____

_____

_____4) **Major commitment** to the other person's welfare — be *loyal*

_____

_____

_____5) Offering **spiritual guidance**/discipleship, deciding to follow Jesus. Be *sharing/caring*

_____

_____

_____6) Help them move from being self-centered to **others-centered** — *making disciples*

_____

_____

_____7) Coaching/training them to be a spiritual grandparent — *reproducing disciples*

_____

_____

_____8) Doing people **planning t**o reach out as a group — *Jesus community/Church*

_____

_____

ABOUT THE AUTHOR

Someone could easily say, "If you were to look up the term 'jack-of-all-trades' in *Webster's Illustrated Dictionary* you would find a picture of Doug Koenigsberg staring back at you!" Really? Yes, really!

Koenigsberg is a man of many talents, personal interests, educational diversity, and expansive vocational and social experiences. His life has been as colorful and complex in design as looking through a kaleidoscope.

As a young man, Doug acquired a college degree in English and Journalism, and went on to spend nearly 20 years as a Minister on a college campus. Today, his passions include, God, family, people, and flying...a topic that he became enamored with as a youth.

Doug earned his Private Pilot's License (PPL) between his junior and senior years of high school. Later, he went on to receive his Commercial Pilot's License (CPL) on single and multi-engine craft, with Instrument Rating. He is currently constructing his 6th experimental airplane project, having had an import business that marketed and sold kit-built airplanes.

Most people seem to be skilled with either their heads or their hands. Doug is reasonably skilled with both, and has a high dose of initiative and motivation to go along with it. So far he has acquired a Commercial Driver license (with motorcycle), a Plumbing License, a Gas Fitter License, a Real Estate License, an HVAC certification, and a Master Service Agent with all the major water heater manufacturers at some point in time. He has been a property "rehabber", conducted a start-up sales initiative in roofing, epoxy flooring and Multi-Level Marketing businesses. He was also a city landlord, and currently has run his own small corporation for nearly 30 years.

Doug's ability to problem-solve, observe and synthesize are his go-to strengths. He typically takes a different starting point than other people, connecting his observations and propositions in a different sequence than the rest of us. This proclivity for unrestricted cause and effect evaluations leads him to consider complex problems and offer refreshing solutions...if they are possible.

Doug made the transition from living in the "all-white" world of the 1960's to being "at-home" in inner-city Baltimore. There was a price to pay however for such a cultural change. Now he bears the marks of prejudice as he often faces rejection by both blacks and whites. Acceptance does occur slowly, but Doug knew this from the beginning.

Of course his wife, Faye, during their 45+ years of marriage, usually takes a deep breath every time Doug comes home with a new idea! Likewise, his three children, Matt, Dan and Beth have grown accustomed to a father whose actions are often difficult to predict as he is always up to something! Fortunately, they are grown, married, and living in their own homes…and made Doug a grandfather of six.

In the church world, Doug is a Presbyterian Elder in the Presbyterian Church USA as well as an Ordained Apostolic Pentecostal Pastor. "It works if you don't ask too many questions", he says. "But in reality, it is about relationships". His devotion to learning the city, doing the work God has lead him to do for over 30 years, has paid off and is illustrated in the contents of this book.

His desire to bring about true fellowship between black and white churches is a driving force in his ministry efforts. He is encouraging white congregations to take the lead by reaching out to include others with cultural differences. This could have the potential to change Sunday services across America…transforming the present day environment from "exclusive to inclusive", and from "segregated to integrated" and all the while, bringing glory to God.

Doug has lived his life serving others since 1965, when as a college freshman, he resolved to spend his life submitted to serve God in ways that benefit others. He seeks to apply the Scripture that says,

"Therefore my beloved brothers, be ye steadfast, immovable, always abounding in the work of the Lord, for you know that your labor is not in vain in the Lord."

I Corinthians 15:58

You may contact the author by email: **cityministrysecrets@gmail.com**
Or follow **cityministrysecrets** on Facebook.